NATIONS *IN TRANSITION*

# VIETNAM

by Tony Zurlo

Jefferson Twp. Public Library
1031 Weldon Road
Oak Ridge, NJ 07438
(973) 208-6115

GREENHAVEN
PRESS ®

THOMSON
™
GALE

San Diego • Detroit • New York • San Francisco • Cleveland
New Haven, Conn. • Waterville, Maine • London • Munich

**THOMSON**

━━━━━✳━━━━━ ™

**GALE**

---

**LIBRARY OF CONGRESS CATALOGING-IN-PUBLICATION DATA**

---

Vietnam / Tony Zurlo, book author.
  p. cm. — (Nations in transition)
Includes bibliographical references and index.
ISBN 0-7377-1214-7 (lib : alk. paper)
  1. Vietnam. I. Zurlo, Tony. II. Nations in transition (Greenhaven Press)
  DS556.3.V46 2004
  959.7—dc21

                                                 2003057963

---

Printed in the United States of America

# Contents

# Foreword

In 1986 Soviet general secretary Mikhail Gorbachev initiated his plan to reform the economic, political, and social structure of the Soviet Union. Nearly three-quarters of a century of Communist ideology was dismantled in the next five years. As the totalitarian regime relaxed its rule and opened itself up to the West, the Soviet peoples clamored for more freedoms. Hard-line Communists resisted Gorbachev's lead, but glasnost, or "openness," could not be stopped with the will of the common people behind it.

In 1991 the changing USSR held its first multicandidate elections. The reform-minded Boris Yeltsin, a supporter of Gorbachev, became the first popularly elected president of the Russian Republic in Soviet history. Under Yeltsin's leadership, the old Communist policies soon all but disintegrated, as did the Soviet Union itself. The Union of Soviet Socialist Republics broke apart into fifteen independent entities. The former republics reformed into a more democratic union now referred to as the Commonwealth of Independent States. Russia remained the nominal figurehead of the commonwealth, but it no longer dictated the future of the other independent states.

By the new millennium, Russia and the other commonwealth states still faced crises. The new states were all in transition from decades of totalitarian rule to the postglasnost era of unprecedented and untested democratic reforms. Revamping the Soviet economy may have opened up new opportunities in private ownership of property and business, but it did not bring overnight prosperity to the former republics. Common necessities such as food still remain in short supply in many regions. And while new governments seek to stabilize their authority, crime rates have escalated throughout the former Soviet Union. Still, the people are confident that their newfound freedoms—freedom of speech and assembly, freedom of religion, and even the right of workers to strike—will ultimately better their lives. The process of change will take time and the people are willing to see their respective states through the challenges of this transitional period in Soviet history.

The collapse and rebuilding of the former Soviet Union provides perhaps the best example of a contemporary "nation in transition," the focus of this Greenhaven Press series. However, other nations that fall under the series rubric have faced a host of unique and varied cultural shifts. India, for instance, is a stable, guiding force in Asia, yet it remains a nation in transition more than fifty years after winning independence from Great Britain. The entire infrastructure of the Indian subcontinent still bears the marking of its colonial past: In a land of eighteen official spoken languages, for example, English remains the voice of politics and education. India is still coming to grips with its colonial legacy while forging its place as a strong player in Asian and world affairs.

North Korea's place in Greenhaven's Nations in Transition series is based on major recent political developments. After decades of antagonism between its Communist government and the democratic leadership of South Korea, tensions seemed to ease in the late 1990s. Even under the shadow of the North's developing nuclear capabilities, the presidents of both North and South Korea met in 2000 to propose plans for possible reunification of the two estranged nations. And though it is one of the three remaining bastions of communism in the world, North Korea is choosing not to remain an isolated relic of the Cold War. While it has not earned the trust of the United States and many of its Western allies, North Korea has begun to reach out to its Asian neighbors to encourage trade and cultural exchanges.

These three countries exemplify the types of changes and challenges that qualify them as subjects of study in the Greenhaven Nations in Transition series. The series examines specific nations to disclose the major social, political, economic, and cultural shifts that have caused massive change and in many cases, brought about regional and/or worldwide shifts in power. Detailed maps, inserts, and pictures help flesh out the people, places, and events that define the country's transitional period. Furthermore, a comprehensive bibliography points readers to other sources that will deepen their understanding of the nation's complex past and contemporary struggles. With these tools, students and casual readers trace both past history and future challenges of these important nations.

# Introduction
## Emerging from the Shadows of War

For much of the past twenty-one hundred years, Vietnam has been a battleground. The long list of contenders fighting for territory and influence includes the Chinese, French, Japanese, and Americans. The Vietnamese (Viets or Kinh) themselves expanded southward during the Middle Ages, nearly annihilating the Cham around the modern-day cities of Hue and Da Nang and driving out the Khmer in the southern half of what is today Vietnam. Civil war between northern and southern factions tore the nation apart in the seventeenth and eighteenth centuries and again in the mid–twentieth century.

This constant fighting for survival molded a martial character that refused to surrender against vastly superior forces. As historian Douglas Pike writes, "Vietnam's past is characterized by a strongly martial spirit tempered by war, invasion, rebellion, insurgency, dissidence, and social sabotage. In their view, the Vietnamese have always lived in an armed camp." [1]

Stretching from the South China Sea on the east to the Gulf of Thailand in the far south, Vietnam's fourteen-hundred-mile coastline has always attracted foreign invaders. The French, attracted by Vietnam's many ports along the shipping route between India and China, colonized Vietnam in the late nineteenth century. Vietnamese nationalist sentiments eventually prevailed, and France withdrew in 1954, leaving Vietnam divided into two independent governments, one in the north and one in the south. Vietnam soon found itself fighting another war as North Vietnam's Communist government battled to take over the non-Communist South. The conflict between the North and South Vietnam would prevent the nation's economy from developing until a decade after the Communists unified Vietnam in 1975.

The transition from decades of war to building a strong peacetime nation was difficult for the Communist leaders. However, in the late 1980s the leaders opened the economy to private enterprise and competition. Today, with nearly two decades of reform secure, Vietnam appears ready to "take off" economically. In addition, Vietnam is rapidly urbanizing. Although still a nation of small farms, the country is changing rapidly because millions of peasants have moved to cities to look for jobs. Nearly 20 percent of Vietnam's population lives in urban areas today, compared to only 10 percent in the early 1980s.

## A Mixture of Western and Communist Influences

Vietnam's urban identity is a mix of traditional Vietnamese culture, complicated by infusions of Marxist-Leninist and Mao Tsetung ideology and European-American economic pragmatism. Despite these foreign influences, however, the Vietnamese leadership resists foreign domination. The Communist government

*Vendors and shoppers crowd a marketplace in Ho Chi Minh City, where Western and Communist influences coexist.*

has a powerful, defensive attitude against foreigners who urge Vietnam to become a carbon copy of Western nations.

Attempts by Vietnam's leaders to counter Western influences lead to a paradoxical blend of communism and international popular culture. Journalist Andrew Lam describes the effects of this mixing of cultures in Ho Chi Minh City (Saigon):

> Two distinct and contradicting realities exist side by side in Vietnam. Red banners hanging between tamarind trees along boulevards glorify the war against the foreign imperial powers and idolize Ho Chi Minh, not far from glaring billboards for Coca Cola and Tiger Beer and Toyota. Noisy public speakers on telephone poles mouthing communist propaganda are being drowned out by stereos that play the likes of the Backstreet Boys and Whitney Houston at high volume.[2]

Ho Chi Minh City has always been a meeting point for a great variety of people from all over Asia. In the seventeenth century,

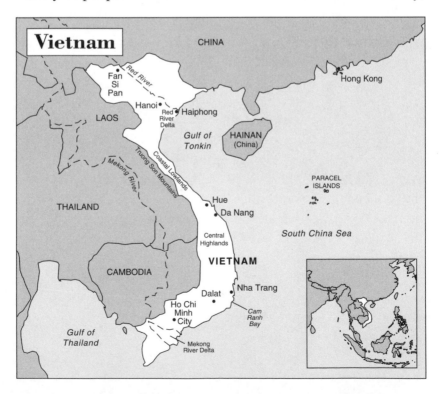

the Viets settled there and began competing with the local Khmers trading with Indians, Malaysians, Japanese, and Chinese. In the late eighteenth century, the Chinese started a marketplace called Cho Lon (Big Market). When the French began to colonize Vietnam in the nineteenth century, they made Ho Chi Minh City the center of their Indo-Chinese empire and built European-style government buildings and homes. They also filled in canals to make new roads. The city became the major port city for the empire.

The people of Ho Chi Minh City have not lost their spirit of capitalist adventurism. As soon as the Communist government declared the economy open for private enterprises in the late 1980s, the city was revitalized as people converted rooms and buildings into restaurants, clothing shops, markets, and other types of businesses. Close to a third of all manufacturing output and retail trade is generated in Ho Chi Minh City.

## The Future

To continue improving its economy, Vietnam needs to expand the vibrant economic activity of Ho Chi Minh City to the rest of the country. With more than 90 percent of its adult population literate, Vietnam is capable of developing more high-tech industries, which in turn will lead to better salaries and higher living standards for the people.

To develop its economy, the government needs other nations to open businesses in Vietnam and expand trade with the country. To gain their cooperation, however, Vietnam must continue opening its economy to competition and improving human rights. Already, it has become an active member in the United Nations, the Association of Southeast Asian Nations, the Asia-Pacific Economic Cooperation forum, the International Monetary Fund, and the Asian Development Bank. By 2005 Vietnam hopes to become a full member of the World Trade Organization.

Vietnam has emerged from the shadows of a hundred years of colonial domination and war to stand on its own as an independent nation. After a short but painful struggle to transform itself into a socialist paradise, Vietnamese leaders have realized they need to learn from and adopt capitalist methods to build an economic foundation that will benefit the people.

# Forging an Identity  1

Three important historical periods shaped the Viet into the modern-day nation of Vietnam. In the earliest period, from the second century B.C. to the tenth century A.D., the Chinese ruled. Even though the Vietnamese absorbed major features of Chinese culture during this time, the people resented foreign rule.

The second period, from the tenth century to the mid–nineteenth century, is characterized by Vietnamese independence from the Chinese and expansion southward into the land that makes up modern Vietnam. During this expansion the Vietnamese developed a strong sense of nationhood. For a short period the country was divided into two semi-independent states north and south of the seventeenth parallel, both claiming allegiance to the Vietnamese emperor. The country was united again in 1802, after a thirty-year civil war.

The third major period began soon after the French took control of Vietnam during the second half of the nineteenth century. Again, the Vietnamese absorbed aspects of the ruling nation's culture while all the time resisting French control.

## The Chinese Millennium

Until the third century B.C., the Viet lived in the Red River Delta and in southern China. They called themselves the Van Lang kingdom. Between 221 B.C. and 206 B.C., a heroic Viet named Thuc Phan repelled a series of Chinese invasions and declared himself king. He renamed the country Au Lac. However, the Viets eventually fell to the Chinese in 111 B.C. The Han dynasty sent in troops and government officials to govern Au Lac as part of China.

The Chinese forced the Viet leaders to prove their loyalty to China's emperor every few years by sending tribute—presents of gold, silver, ivory, spices, silk, crafts, and other supplies—acknowledging China's power. If they failed to pay, the Chinese would send troops to force payment.

During the thousand years of Chinese rule, the Vietnamese upper class absorbed many features of Chinese culture. The Chinese introduced their language, system of writing, Confucian philosophy, and civil service exam system for selecting government officials. Vietnamese landowners adopted Confucian values and other

## The Trung Sisters: A.D. 40–43

Every year, about a month after Tet (New Year's Day), Vietnam celebrates National Woman's Day. The celebration is usually in March, but the date varies because it is determined by the lunar calendar. The holiday commemorates the death of Vietnam's first two national heroes, Trung Trac and Trung Nhi, twin sisters who rallied the Vietnamese people in A.D. 39 to overthrow the Chinese who had occupied their land.

When Trung Trac's husband led an insurrection to restore Vietnamese rule, the Chinese ruler executed him and raped Trac. In response, the sisters organized neighboring tribal lords to overthrow the Chinese. Scholar Danuta Bois describes their short but glorious military career:

> [The sisters] formed an army of about 80,000 men and women. Thirty-six of the generals were women, including the Trung sisters' mother.
>
> The Trung sisters led their army in an attack on the Chinese forces occupying their land. They won back the territory extending from Hue into southern China and they were proclaimed co-queens. Their royal court was established in Me-linh, an ancient political center in the Hong River plain.
>
> In the year 42 C.E. [A.D.], the Chinese forces were sent to recapture the region. The queens and their people fought hard to resist the invader. . . . However, in the end the Vietnamese troops were defeated. According to the popular belief, the Trung sisters elected to take their own lives in the traditional manner: by jumping into a river and drowning. . . . The Trung sisters became symbols of the first Vietnamese resistance to the Chinese occupation of their land. Temples were later built in their honor and the people of Vietnam celebrate their memory every year with a national holiday.

Chinese customs as a way of demonstrating their superiority over the common people.

Although they adopted some Chinese customs, the Vietnamese resented being ruled by a foreign power. The Vietnamese rebelled many times, but their attacks were quelled by the Chinese. Finally, in the late tenth century, a powerful Vietnamese general defeated an invading Chinese fleet. The Chinese had to withdraw, but it took another thirty years of fighting among a dozen different warlords before one Vietnamese general emerged victorious. For the first time in more than a thousand years, Vietnam was unified by General Dinh Bo Linh, who called his nation Dai Co Viet. The new country consisted of most of the region between Hanoi and the southern border with China.

## The Chinese Influence on Vietnam

Even after breaking free from Chinese control, the Vietnamese continued to be strongly influenced by Chinese culture and even modeled their system of government after China's. In the eleventh century the Vietnamese founded a university to educate candidates who would take competitive examinations on Confucian philosophy to qualify for political offices. Chinese influence in Vietnam continued through the centuries and reached a peak during Vietnam's last imperial dynasty, the Nguyen dynasty (1802–1945).

Between 1802 and 1830, the first two Nguyen emperors built a "Forbidden City" in the city of Hue to house his family and court. The Forbidden City was modeled after the walled city in Beijing, China. Vietnamese government officials had to wear Chinese-style gowns, and women were required to wear Chinese-style slacks. The emperor declared a new law code, modeled after China's code, which declared that women were subservient to men. In addition, the first Nguyen emperor revived the use of Chinese written characters in business and education.

## Vietnamese Expansion

The second major factor that shaped modern-day Vietnam was a long period of territorial expansion. During a period of about eight hundred years, the Viet drove other smaller ethnic groups off

*During the early nineteenth century, the first Nguyen emperors built the Forbidden City (pictured) in the city of Hue.*

the land and became the dominant people in the area from the Chinese border southward to the Gulf of Thailand.

Expansion began during the eleventh century, when the Viet began to defend southern Vietnam against raiders from the militant kingdom of Champa, which consisted of the area between modern-day Hue and Da Nang. As they fought their way southward, Vietnamese soldiers settled land in the conquered territories to grow rice. Although it took them several centuries, the Vietnamese had annihilated the Champa kingdom by the fifteenth century. Historian Bernard B. Fall writes that by the early seventeenth century "the Champa kingdom had simply disappeared."[3]

After conquering the Champa kingdom, the Vietnamese continued to expand toward the south, where they faced the Khmer (Cambodian) people. The southeastern edge of the Khmer kingdom was located near the Mekong Delta. However, the Khmer kings were unable to defend this area, and by the mid–seventeenth century the Vietnamese occupied the entire area of present-day western and southern Vietnam.

The Vietnamese gained control of the entire Khmer kingdom by the nineteenth century, and the Khmer king was forced to pay tribute to the Vietnamese emperor. The Vietnamese tried to force the Khmer to adopt Vietnamese culture. Fall writes that the Khmer had to wear Vietnamese clothing and hairstyles, that cities and provinces were given Vietnamese names, and that from 1834 to 1841 the Khmer queen was "held a virtual prisoner in her palace."[4] Only after the French moved in during the last half of the nine-

## *Chinh Nghia:* A Vietnamese Fighting Tradition

The citizen-warrior has a long tradition in Vietnam. The willingness of the common people to take up arms against enemies is attributed to a national characteristic called *chinh nghia,* or "just cause." Historian Douglas Pike explains this tradition in *Vietnam: Countries of the World:*

> Contemporary Hanoi historians . . . cite the famed historical record, Annam Chu Luoc (*Description of Annam,* by Le Tac, circa 1340): "During the Tran dynasty all the people fought the enemy. Everyone was a soldier, which is why they were able to defeat the savage enemy. This is the general experience throughout the people's entire history." This tradition is said to arise not from militarism, but rather from a spirit of chinh nghia (just cause), which connotes highly moral behavior rooted in rationality, compassion, and responsibility. The historians assert that the spirit of chinh nghia sustained the Vietnamese in their long struggle against the Sinicization (Han-hwa) efforts of the Han Chinese, and later against French colonialism and American neocolonialism. Drawn from this, then, is a special kind of martial spirit, both ferocious and virtuous. It is because of chinh nghia that the Vietnamese have been victorious, while usually outnumbered and outgunned. Chinh nghia is the mystique that imparts unique fighting capabilities to the Vietnamese: first, it mobilizes the people and turns every inhabitant into a soldier; second, it applies the principles of "knowing how to fight the strong by the weak, the great numbers by the small numbers, the large by the small."

teenth century did the Vietnamese withdraw from Cambodia and northern Laos.

## Civil War

As Vietnam expanded southward, powerful rival families became more and more independent from the royal government in Hue. Between 1533 and 1788 the political and economic affairs of the nation were controlled by two powerful families: the Trinh in the northern half (from Quang Tri province to the Chinese border) and the Nguyen family in the southern half. To keep the Trinh family from invading, the Nguyens built a wall twenty feet high and eleven miles long near the city of Dong-Hoi.

While the Trinh and Nguyen families ruled semi-independent states, the nation's economy deteriorated. Millions of homeless peasants rioted, demanding food and land reform. As many as one-third of all the villages in the north were abandoned during the mid–eighteenth century because the peasants were unable to grow enough crops to pay their debts. New taxes were placed on items that people used in their daily lives, such as charcoal for cooking and heat, salt for preserving food, and silk for clothing. In addition, the extensive irrigation network was neglected by the government, leading to floods and starvation. As a result, tens of thousands of people abandoned their land and wandered the countryside in search of food. This suffering led to frequent peasant revolts during the mid–eighteenth century.

The revolts protesting the miserable conditions culminated in the Tay Son rebellion, begun in 1771 by three brothers from the village of Tay Son in Nghe An province in north-central Vietnam. They were committed to helping the poor throughout the country by attacking wealthy landowners and elitist officials. Their main targets were landlords who exploited the peasants and corrupt scholar-officials. The brothers redistributed their lands. In addition, the brothers released local prisoners, eliminated most taxes, and gave food stored in government storehouses to the people.

By 1789 the Tay Son brothers controlled what is today modern Vietnam. One brother, Hue, declared himself emperor of a unified Vietnam. However, after his death in 1792 the remaining Tay Son

*This shrine in the Hue Museum honors the leaders of the Tay Son rebellion.*

brothers were unable to maintain control. In the south, the only surviving male of the former ruling Nguyen family, Nguyen Anh, returned from hiding with an army and a steady supply of munitions from the French government. Civil war continued for another decade before Nguyen Anh was able to defeat the Tay Son. In 1802 Nguyen declared himself emperor of Vietnam, taking the name Gia Long.

## A Fragile Unity

Even though Vietnam remained under a unified administration during Gia Long's reign, thousands of corrupt government officials refused to obey him. Gia Long complained that the recalcitrant bureaucrats "regard laws as empty text, resorting to all tricks to make money, otherwise the innocent will be accused of guilt."[5] Gia Long was unable to control corruption, and the mandarins and landlords became richer.

Under Gia Long's rule, the peasants suffered greatly. In addition to facing natural disasters such as floods and typhoons, the peasants were heavily taxed. Tax payments took the form of work and crops and enabled the government to build imperial tombs, town walls, public roads, and canals. Tens of thousands of peasants died on these projects. In response to the harsh conditions, teams of workers would strike or join rebel groups that challenged the government's authority. During the first half of the nineteenth century, thousands of uprisings broke out against emperors Gia Long and his successor, Ming Manh (reigned 1820–1840). By the mid–nineteenth century, the Nguyen royal family was losing control of the nation.

# French Colonialism

During this long period of civil war and tenuous unity, the French arrived in Southeast Asia hoping to engage in trade and spread the belief in Christianity. They were also looking for spices, gold, and other materials. Christian missionaries accounted for most of the early European contact with the Vietnamese and found early success in converting the people. As early as 1640, approximately 120,000 Vietnamese had become Christians. The number of Vietnamese Christians expanded to about 300,000 by 1830 and 600,000 by 1850. Vietnamese Christians often established their own villages, set up Christian schools, and created local governments in defiance of Confucian authority. In response, Ming Manh ordered imprisonment and sometimes death for anyone preaching or practicing Christianity.

The missionaries appealed to the French government for help. Realizing that protecting missionaries would also make for safer and more profitable trade, France sent a navy fleet to the South China Sea in 1841 as a show of force. When Tu Duc (reigned 1847–1883) took the throne, he learned that French missionaries were scheming with his enemies to overthrow him. In retaliation he declared that Vietnamese Christians who refused to renounce their faith would lose their citizenship. He also stepped up the arrest and punishment of European missionaries. When he had a Spanish bishop executed in 1857, France and Spain joined efforts to send a Spanish naval expedition to Da Nang.

# France Takes Control of the South

During the nineteenth century, European nations were competing for colonies in Africa and Asia with plans to extract minerals and use the port cities to expand their trade. Because the Spanish were more interested in the Philippines, they withdrew their forces and small contingent of missionaries from Da Nang. The French, on the other hand, stayed in hopes of establishing a colony there. However, their casualties from the heat and disease in Da Nang were high, causing the French to withdraw as well.

Still hoping to establish a colony in Southeast Asia, the French decided to occupy Gia Dinh, near the Mekong Delta, which would provide France with a deep-water port for trade. Occupying the city in 1859, they renamed it Saigon. Meanwhile, Tu Duc decided he could not fight the French while subduing uprisings in the north. As a result, he signed the Treaty of Saigon in 1862, ceding three southeastern provinces in the Mekong Delta to the French. The French renamed their new colony Cochinchina. Tu Duc also agreed to open three more ports to the French and to allow Catholics to practice their religion.

Despite the treaty, Vietnamese resistance to foreign rule led to guerrilla warfare against the French in the south. Admiral Bonard, France's commander in charge of Cochinchina, reported, "We have had enormous difficulties in enforcing our authority. . . . Rebel bands disturb the country everywhere. They appear from nowhere in large numbers, destroy everything and then disappear into nowhere."[6] In the long run, however, French military power prevailed. In 1863 France extended its control over Cambodia, and in 1867 French troops occupied three more provinces in southern Vietnam.

## France Takes Control of the North

France wanted to initiate trade with China and believed the Red River in the north would provide its merchants with a cheap water route into southern China. The Vietnamese officials had forbidden foreigners from using the river for trade, although several Europeans continued the practice. In 1873 a Frenchman was imprisoned by the Vietnamese authorities for trading on the river. The French governor of Cochinchina sent naval officer Francis Garnier with troops to Hanoi in November 1873 to free the trader. After obtaining the trader's release, Garnier went on to occupy a portion of Hanoi and five other port cities and claimed the northern half of Vietnam for France.

The French had no taste for the fierce resistance that followed. A paramilitary gang of Chinese and Vietnamese outlaws called the Black Flags joined forces with the emperor's troops to defend the north. They killed Garnier in battle and recaptured the ports. In 1874 the French and Vietnamese signed a treaty whereby the French were to withdraw troops from Hanoi in exchange for use of the Red River and two ports, and the emperor was to recognize France's authority over Cochinchina. The agreement also allowed the French to establish businesses and build government residences in selected cities.

Vietnamese nationalists, including the Black Flags, rioted against the treaty. The French reacted by sending troops under Captain Henri Revière to Hanoi in May 1883. By defeating opponents of the treaty, the French believed they could claim the northern part of Vietnam as a colony. Revière was killed in battle, but the French refused to withdraw. In August a French naval fleet bombarded Hue into submission. The final treaty in 1884 forced the emperor to recognize France's rule over all of Vietnam.

## French Indochina

In 1887 France created the Indochinese Union, composed of protectorates and colonies. The protectorates of Annam (central Vietnam), Tonkin (northern Vietnam), Cambodia, and Laos (established in 1893) retained their traditional leaders, but French officials supervised them closely. Each of the colonies—Cochinchina, Da Nang, Haiphong, and Hanoi—were placed under the direct rule of a French governor or mayor. Government assemblies with Vietnamese representatives were formed, but only as forums for discussion. French advisers at all governmental levels controlled policy.

The expense of operating the territories immediately drained the French treasury. Paying the salaries of thousands of French bureaucrats recruited to run the territorial governments took up nearly half of the French budget. Another major portion of the budget went toward constructing roads, digging canals, modernizing Hanoi and Saigon, and preparing

*French soldiers quell a nationalist riot in Hanoi in 1883.*

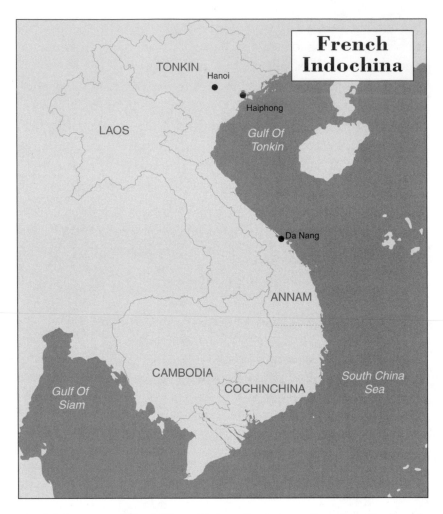

the Mekong and Red River Deltas for international trade. In addition, the French developed and expanded ports at cities such as Da Nang and Hong Gai.

In 1897 France sent former French minister of finance Paul Doumer to serve as governor-general of the Indochinese Union with a mandate to make the union profitable for France. To raise money, Doumer declared a government monopoly on the production and marketing of alcohol, salt, and opium. These products quickly accounted for 70 percent of the government's revenue. Historian Alexander Woodside describes the process: "[Peasants] had to obtain government permits to make wine, after which they had to sell the wine they made to the government, which sold it back to them through licensed French retailers at a profit."[7] This same process applied to salt and opium. Opium and alcohol houses were built in most villages throughout the country to encourage consumption. The opium business proved to be the most profitable, accounting for 33 percent of the colonial government's revenue during Doumer's term (1897–1902).

## Economic Exploitation

The French colonial government found other ways to raise revenue. The most profitable was taxes on rice and rubber exports. In the past, emperors had prohibited rice exports, choosing instead to store the surplus for distribution during emergencies. However,

*Workers pour rubber sap into large tanks. By the early 1900s, rubber had become one of Vietnam's most profitable exports.*

the French turned rice into their most profitable export crop. To increase production, the French reclaimed large areas of land in the Mekong Delta and took land from peasants who defaulted on taxes and loans. The government then sold the land to investors to cultivate. Only the French were allowed to buy up most of it. A few Vietnamese who cooperated with French officials were allowed to buy land, but 90 percent of the plantations were French owned. As a result of this French system, more than 70 percent of the peasants in Cochinchina were landless by 1930. Now they had to work as hired plantation workers or tenant farmers and pay 40 to 70 percent of their harvest to work the farmland. By the 1930s, landless peasants made up about 50 percent of Vietnam's population.

The second most important export product was rubber. In the 1920s the amount of land dedicated to rubber plantations increased fourteen times to 250,000 square acres. French companies such as Compagnie des Terres Rouges, Mimot, and Michelin expanded their rubber exports from two hundred tons in 1914 to more than ten thousand tons by 1930.

The companies paid little attention to plantation working and living conditions. Workers who survived the intense heat and humidity often suffered from malaria, cholera, dysentery, and other diseases. They found no relief back at their thatched, leaky barracks. Historian Cecil B. Currey writes that workers were often "packed so tight [in the barracks] many were forced to sleep seated, more than a few of them shaking with the chills of malarial fever."[8] Death became so common on the plantations that people referred to workers as fertilizer for the rubber trees.

The French also took control of the coal, silver, gold, copper, and tin mines in Vietnam. The area being mined expanded from about 152,500 square acres before World War I to 1.07 million square acres by the early 1920s. Profits for French companies were enormous. The owners of the Northern Coal Company doubled their investment during the 1920s. In the Hong Gai coal mines of northeast Vietnam, the output expanded from .5 million tons to 2 million tons between 1913 and 1927. By 1930 about fifty thousand Vietnamese worked in the mines. The working conditions in the mines were just as horrendous as on the rubber plantations.

# The Distribution of Wealth Among the Vietnamese

Most Vietnamese suffered from poverty during the colonial period. The few thousand Vietnamese who were wealthy were mostly absentee landlords with large holdings in the Mekong Delta. Another group of Vietnamese entered the middle and upper classes during World War II by opening small businesses and industries such as print shops, textile weaving and rice milling plants, and cement and brick-making factories. By the mid-1930s approximately 10 percent of the population of 18 million had attained enough wealth to be considered middle or upper class. Many of these were high school and college graduates who worked as engineers, bankers, agronomists, and doctors. Another group consisted of the lower-level civil servants.

To maintain their superior positions, the French instituted a two-tier wage system. French workers got a much higher salary for performing the same jobs as Vietnamese workers. French workers with low-level jobs requiring no education were better paid than Vietnamese with higher qualifications and responsibilities. Historian Bernard B. Fall writes in his book *The Two Viet-Nams* that "the French janitor at the University of Hanoi received a base pay that was slightly higher than that of a Vietnamese professor with a Ph.D. from the University of Paris."[9]

# The Seeds of Resistance

By the time the French arrived, the Vietnamese had developed a strong sense of nationalism. They had overcome a thousand years of Chinese rule to assert themselves as a unified nation. They had overrun smaller kingdoms to the south and consolidated the entire landmass between China and the Gulf of Thailand. On the other hand, Western economic and political ideas had changed Vietnam's society profoundly. French entrepreneurs introduced modern methods of business and industrial production. Thousands of Vietnamese traveled to Europe for education and work, and most of them returned with dreams of making their country economically and politically independent.

# The Struggle for Independence 2

Two different viewpoints dominated the Vietnamese nationalist movement in the early twentieth century. The group led by Phan Boi Chau argued for violence to overthrow colonialism while the group led by Phan Chau Trinh sought French guidance toward peaceful independence. The French reacted to Vietnamese efforts toward independence with an iron hand, arresting tens of thousands of demonstrators and nationalist spokespersons such as Chau and Trinh.

After World War I, protesters in Vietnam began demonstrating for better working conditions. This labor unrest in the cities drew the attention of the Communist International (Comintern), a Moscow-based organization that supervised Communist parties around the world and supported revolutions against the colonial governments in Asia, Africa, and the Middle East.

The man most responsible for taking advantage of working-class discontent was Ho Chi Minh. Only twenty when he left Vietnam in 1911, Ho visited several nations before settling down in Paris in 1917. He was convinced that the capitalist Western nations would never help the Vietnamese gain their independence. However, the new Communist government of the Union of Soviet Socialist Republics (USSR) was calling for a worldwide war against colonialism. Therefore, Ho traveled to Moscow and joined the Comintern so he could get support for his plans to lead a revolution back in Vietnam.

For several years Ho moved back and forth between Paris and Moscow, evading the French secret police who wanted to question him about his Comintern connections. When Ho moved to China in the mid-1920s on Comintern business, he had to keep hiding because the anti-Communist Chinese government under Chiang Kai-shek wanted to arrest him.

## The Communist Party in Indochina

While living in Guangzhou, China, Ho Chi Minh formed the Revolutionary Youth League (RYL), a Communist-oriented organization for Vietnamese nationalists. In the RYL's journal *Youth,* Ho introduced a simplified version of Marxism that quickly attracted attention. RYL membership grew from three hundred in 1928 to more than seventeen hundred a year later.

As an extension of the RYL, Ho started a political school to teach recruits how to lead the masses against the French. His teachings emphasized proper attitude and behavior in dealing with the masses. Students were taught to maintain a strong moral character throughout the coming fight for independence. Another key personal quality they learned, according to historian William J. Duiker, was "how to behave without condescension to the poor and illiterate." [10] After four months of study, students returned to Vietnam as underground agents of revolution.

*Ho Chi Minh led the Vietnamese people in their fight for independence.*

In May 1929 seventeen RYL delegates held their first congress in Hong Kong. Some delegates wanted to form an official Communist party, but others argued that RYL members first needed more education in Marxism. Delegates ended up splitting into three separate Communist parties. The Comintern stepped in and placed the three Vietnamese parties under the supervision of the Chinese Communist Party. Because the Comintern believed that a divided Communist movement in Vietnam would be ineffective, it placed the three

Vietnamese parties under the supervision of the Chinese Communist Party. However, Ho was determined to keep the Vietnamese Communists independent. He therefore created a single Vietnamese Communist Party in 1930 to satisfy the Comintern. The Comintern changed the name to the Indochinese Communist Party (ICP) so that it could include the colonized people in Cambodia and Laos.

In 1930 Ho published ten goals for the party that included independence for all parts of Indochina; a "worker-peasant-soldier government"[11]; government confiscation of land, banks, and businesses; a shorter workday; elimination of unfair taxes; free education for everyone; and equality of the sexes.

## The Rebellions of 1930

Many of the ICP leaders risked arrest by returning to Vietnam. Ho remained in hiding in China. In the meantime, another anticolonial

---

### Ho Chi Minh's Leadership

One reason Ho Chi Minh succeeded as leader of the Vietnamese revolution was his uncanny ability to evade his enemies. He could blend in with crowds and take on multiple disguises. He lived under more than a dozen aliases and passed safely in numerous disguises, including as a peasant, a Chinese journalist, a Buddhist monk, and a Roman Catholic priest.

Ho Chi Minh also possessed extraordinary diplomatic skills. Against the eagerness of many revolutionaries during the 1930s and 1940s to confront the French head-on, Ho counseled for caution. His followers respected him because he had paid his dues as an active worker for the Comintern throughout Europe, in Russia, and in China.

Ho seems to have impressed most people as genuinely lacking in pretension. He was not pushy or arrogant, despite his strong intelligence and many achievements. People, ranging from his own Vietnamese admirers to the Americans with the Office of Strategic Services during World War II, seemed to truly like him. Although staunch anti-Communists such as Chinese Nationalist leader Chiang Kai-shek and South Vietnam's Ngo Dinh Diem never trusted him, Ho drew many non-Communists to his cause because of his disarming personality. By World War II, Ho had become a respected elder in his colleagues' eyes.

political party was launching terrorist activities in Vietnam. In 1929 the Viet Nam Quoc Dan Dang (VNQDD), or Vietnam Nationalist Party, assassinated the French supervisor of labor recruitment for rubber plantations. The colonial government arrested several hundred party members in retaliation, but the VNQDD's leaders responded by calling for the approximately fifteen thousand Vietnamese troops serving the French at military garrisons to mutiny. The French used airpower to crush the rebellions, and most of the VNQDD leaders were executed.

Against Ho's advice, the ICP entered into the fray. On May 1, 1930, ICP-led demonstrations against the French exploded into riots throughout Annam. A period of chaos and killing followed, called the "Red Terror" by the French. Angry crowds took over villages, set up Communist governments, seized and redistributed land, tortured and punished landlords, and killed many innocent people. In September 1930 six thousand peasants and workers marched on Vinh, the capital of Nghe An province, demanding economic reforms. The French once again called in airpower to attack marchers stretched along two miles of highway, killing more than two hundred and wounding many more.

The French rapidly destroyed the latest Communist uprising. The Vietnamese refer to this period as the "White Terror." Whole villages were destroyed. The colonial government rounded up about seventy thousand suspected leaders of Communist and nationalist groups and either imprisoned or exiled them. Another seven hundred Vietnamese were executed. In all, more than ten thousand people were killed during the 1930 disturbances.

## Ho Chi Minh Returns to Vietnam

Instead of advancing the cause of independence, the ICP's premature rebellions weakened the independence movement, as Ho had predicted. The French arrested and imprisoned much of the Communist leadership. When Ho traveled to Hong Kong in 1933, French colonial officials convinced the British to arrest him. However, with the secret help of two sympathetic British officials, Ho escaped to China. From there he moved to Moscow, where he taught communism and mentored Vietnamese students. In 1938 the Comintern sent Ho to southern China to report back on the Chinese Communists' activities. However, German and Japanese military aggression interrupted his work. When France surrendered to Germany during the beginning of World War II in June 1940, Ho told the editorial board of the ICP newspaper *D.T.* that "the French defeat represents a very favorable opportunity for the Vietnamese revolution. We must seek every means to return home to take advantage of it. To delay would be harmful to the revolution." [12]

Ho immediately opened a military camp in Jingxi, China, to train Vietnamese to fight the French. He also created the League for the Independence of Vietnam, or Vietminh, which recruited nationalists from many different political groups. On February 8, 1941, Ho crossed the border into the mountains of Vietnam and established his headquarters near Pac Bo in Caobang province, inside a huge cave surrounded by jungle growth and limestone cliffs. In this cave on May 10, 1941, Ho presided over the Eighth Plenum (meeting) of the ICP's Central Committee, which ratified his plans for the revolution against the French.

Ho named Vo Nguyen Giap to lead the Vietminh army. After intensive training, Giap's cadres (political-military leaders) spread out into villages to recruit others to their cause. Once villages had been won over, the cadres would establish a local government and move on to neighboring villages. Soon they controlled much of Caobang province in northeastern Vietnam.

## Japanese Forces in Vietnam

The Vietminh's ability to carry out revolution was complicated by the arrival of the Japanese, who were allies with Nazi Germany. When the Germans had invaded France, a group of French in the city of Vichy, claiming to be the legitimate French government, collaborated with Germany. As a result, the French colonial government in Indochina had to cooperate with Germany's ally, Japan. Although Japan allowed France to continue ruling Vietnam, the French had to agree to Japanese military occupation. Before long, thirty-five thousand Japanese troops were stationed in central and northern Vietnam. Before the end of World War II, the Japanese had an additional one hundred thousand troops in Cochinchina.

# Vo Nguyen Giap

Vo Nguyen Giap commanded the Communist military through thirty-five years of war, from 1940 to 1975. After World War II he also served as Ho Chi Minh's minister of defense. The two men frequently clashed over Ho's more moderate approach to revolution, but they trusted each other thoroughly. Although Giap carried out Communist Party decisions in the war against South Vietnam, he often opposed the majority's call for conventional warfare. He preferred an extensive guerrilla campaign before a general attack. Historian Cecil B. Currey describes Giap as a highly intelligent man but one who guarded his reputation with a temper.

> Giap was a man of extensive culture, gifted with an encyclopedic intelligence, a product of the university. He was the only member of the [Vietnamese Communist Party] Politburo with an advanced, essentially western intellectual background. He did not always concern himself with details. He was enthusiastic, emotional, and dramatic. He was a partisan and advocate of spectacular and imaginative actions, with little regard for resultant consequences or losses. He was usually a direct man and, when angry, prone to say whatever was on his mind. Giap was very sensitive with respect to matters affecting his own prestige, and receptive to compliments and flattery while resentful of criticism. As he gained authority within the Viet Minh movement, and particularly after he became head of the army, Giap resisted all attempts to place any control upon his command.

*Military commander Vo Nguyen Giap inspects members of the People's Army of Vietnam in 1952.*

When Japan's empire in the Pacific began to collapse, Japanese leaders tried to hold on to Vietnam by abolishing the French colonial government on March 9, 1945. Japan declared the northern and central parts of Vietnam the independent Kingdom of Annam under the rule of Emperor Bao Dai, a descendant of the Nguyen dynasty. In reality, Annam was a puppet state under Japan's control.

Japan's ability to control Vietnam had deteriorated, however, because wartime conditions caused the economy in the north to fall apart. Hundreds of thousands of people in the countryside survived by eating roots and tree bark. As famine continued unabated, nearly 2 million out of a population of 10 million had died by the summer of 1945. General Giap reported the disaster along the major route north of Hanoi: "There were not enough garbage carts to carry the corpses of those who had died of starvation to the suburbs to dump them in mass graves. Meanwhile, starving masses of people were still pouring in through the city gates from the countryside. They staggered and wandered like dry leaves falling on a winter evening." [13]

## *Doc Lap*—Independence

In the spring of 1945 the Vietminh began their drive to take over Vietnam's government. General Giap and other Vietnamese nationalist leaders formed the People's Liberation Army (PLA), also known as the Vietnam Liberation Army. The army had little trouble taking over territory in the north, where it created people's revolutionary committees to govern at the village, district, and provincial levels. The committees confiscated land from the French and distributed it to poor farmers, set up literacy classes, and formed self-defense militias.

While the Vietminh were quickly taking over the north, the United States, USSR, and Great Britain decided that Japan's surrender and disarmament in Vietnam would be supervised not by Vietnamese but rather by Chinese troops in the north and British troops in the south. Ho was upset and vowed to have his own independent government in place before the Allied forces arrived.

When the Japanese surrendered to the United States on August 14, 1945, the ICP made its move. The ICP Central Committee immediately declared Vietnam independent under the name of the Democratic Republic of Vietnam (DRVN). The committee elected Ho chairman of the five-man National Liberation Committee to serve as a provisional government until Giap's army could drive out the Japanese. On August 16 Giap's main forces moved toward Hanoi. With very little resistance from the Japanese, Giap's troops entered Hanoi on August 19. Two hundred thousand cheering Vietnamese welcomed the troops. In a note to French president Charles de Gaulle, Bao Dai, the longtime puppet of both the French and the Japanese, tried to explain his people's elation:

> You could understand even better [the people's joy] . . . if you were able to sense the desire for independence that has been smoldering in the bottom of all hearts, and which no human force can any longer hold back. Even if you were to arrive to reestablish a French administration here, it would no longer be obeyed; each village would be a nest of resistance, every former friend an enemy. [14]

In the south, however, the Vietminh were not given such a warm welcome. Troops from non-Communist armed militias opposed the Vietminh's claim to speak for all Vietnamese. Additional opposition came from the large anti-Communist middle class in the Saigon and Mekong Delta areas. Some of those opposed to the Vietminh formed the National United Front to take over local governments.

Most southern Vietminh leaders had been killed or were in prison. However, Tran Van Giau, who had escaped in 1941, returned as an official with the ICP's southern branch, which controlled the million-member Vanguard Youth organization and the Vietnam Trade Union. On August 20, 1945, he created the Committee of the South (COS) and served as its first chairman. Five days later, a COS-sponsored militia took over government installations in Saigon, and by noon Giau was in control of the city.

With both the north and the south under Vietminh control, Ho entered Hanoi to prepare the first independent Vietnamese government in almost eighty years. Emperor Bao Dai cooperated with Ho and abdicated the throne. On September 2, 1945, Ho officially declared Vietnam's independence to a gathering of 1 million people in Hanoi's Ba Dinh Square. It was a bold attempt to assert Vietnamese sovereignty.

## The French Return

Both the south and the north were now under ICP control, but not for long. In the north, 150,000 Chinese troops were arriving

## Ho Chi Minh's Declaration of Independence

Under a bright, sunny sky on September 2, 1945, flags, lanterns, flowers, red bunting, and other kinds of decorations were flapping in the breeze throughout the city. Close to a million peasants and workers, some in plain dress and others in colorful traditional costumes and robes, danced and sang in the streets as they waited for Ho Chi Minh to appear at Ba Dinh Square. Just after 2:00 P.M., General Giap introduced their nation's new leader. Dressed in a borrowed khaki suit and high-collared jacket, Ho mounted a fifteen-foot rostrum and waited while the crowd chanted "*Doc lap*," or "Independence." Finally, Ho presented a short, emotional declaration. His respect for American and French ideals were clear in his Declaration of Independence of the Democratic Republic of Viet Nam speech:

> All men are created equal. They are endowed by their Creator with certain unalienable Rights; among these are Life, Liberty and the pursuit of Happiness.

> This immortal statement appeared in the Declaration of Independence of the United States of America in 1776. In a broader sense, it means: All the peoples on the earth are equal from birth, all the peoples have a right to live and to be happy and free.

> The Declaration of the Rights of Man and the Citizen, made at the time of the French Revolution, in 1791, also states: "All men are born free and with equal rights, and must always remain free and have equal rights.

> Those are undeniable truths.

to disarm the Japanese. And in the south, 5,000 British troops were in place, soon to be followed by tens of thousands of French soldiers.

In Saigon, the British commander Major General Douglas Gracey released fourteen hundred French prisoners of war. They immediately rampaged through the streets, attacking Vietnamese bystanders. After Gracey restored order, he evicted Giau's COS government. Soon General Jacques Philippe Leclerc arrived as commander of France's Far East forces and declared, "We have come to claim our inheritance." [15] Clearly the French intended to restore their colonial empire to prewar status. After a short fight, the French controlled Saigon; Bao Dai once again became a puppet leader. No match for the French military in open battle, the Vietminh reverted to guerrilla tactics in the south.

# Ho Chi Minh's First National Government

The French had regained control of the south, but the Vietminh controlled the northern half of Vietnam. France, however, was posed for the right moment to send troops back into the north to reestablish French rule. In an attempt to rally non-Communists to his side, Ho Chi Minh appointed ten non-Communists to his sixteen-member cabinet. He also abolished the ICP. However, the Communist Party continued to meet and organize secretly, and its members continued to dominate political affairs in the north. Ho announced plans for nationwide legislative elections on January 6, 1946. Because non-Communists complained that the elections would be unfair, Ho promised that his government would offer fifty seats to the VNQDD and twenty to the Dong Minh Hoi (DMH) Party.

The Vietminh, under Communist guidance, won 97 percent of the popular vote. However, when the new National Assembly met on March 2 with 333 members, Ho convinced the assembly to accept the 70 appointed members of the VNQDD and DMH as a show of Vietnamese unity.

Despite Ho's attempt to create a somewhat inclusive government, his enemies complained that the Vietminh controlled the elections around the country. One candidate who ran against the Vietminh, Nguyen Duy Thanh, alleged that the Communists had unfairly manipulated the proceedings:

> In my home village the polling secretary was away. . . . The voters could not even see the voting papers. And yet fifteen candidates nominated by the Communist Party were declared duly elected by a thousand votes. . . . [In the south] no election worth the name was held, but the Communists announced that 80 percent of the electorate had voted for ten members of the Communist Party. [16]

## Final Negotiations with the French

Clinging to his dream of Vietnamese independence, Ho signed a tentative agreement with French representative Jean Sainteny in March 1946. France would accept the DRVN's independence if Ho agreed that his government would join the Federation of Indochinese States, a group that would consist of Cambodia, Laos, and Vietnam. In addition, fifteen thousand French troops would replace the Chinese troops still stationed in the north, but they would all be withdrawn within five years. It was the best deal Ho could make.

Ho sailed for France not realizing that the French government never intended to allow any of its former Indo-Chinese possessions true independence. In a move that foreshadowed the French return to the north, Admiral Georges Thierry d'Argenlieu, France's high commissioner in charge of Indochina, declared Cochinchina

*Ho Chi Minh meets with French officials in 1946. After negotiating with the French government, Ho realized that Vietnam would have to fight in order to achieve independence.*

an independent republic within the newly created French Union, a general term that included former colonies and territories. France allowed the "independent republics" in the union limited self-government, but in reality France remained in control of their economies and foreign affairs and supervised their political affairs. D'Argenlieu's move was the first step in creating the Federation of Indochinese States, which would include Cambodia, Laos, and Vietnam, under a single French governor.

Knowing that the Vietnamese people would have to fight to be truly independent, Ho told an American journalist that the Vietnamese would win in the end: "We have a weapon every bit as powerful as the most modern cannon: nationalism! Do not underestimate its power." [17]

## The First Indo-Chinese War Breaks Out

After sporadic fighting between the Vietminh and the French in the fall of 1946, the French seized a Vietnamese fishing vessel they claimed was transporting arms to the Vietnamese guerrillas in Haiphong harbor in November 1946. When the Vietminh fought back, the French shelled Haiphong, killing several thousand Vietnamese. The hostilities spread southward toward Hanoi. A month later, French authorities demanded that the Vietminh surrender their arms and allow French troops to take over public safety in the north. Giap responded by attacking a French garrison in Hanoi, but his troops suffered large casualties. The following day, Ho called for a people's rebellion "to exterminate the enemy and save the country, to fight to the last drop of blood and, whatever the cost, to refuse re-enslavement." [18]

The French took control of Haiphong, Hanoi, and the provincial capitals by early February 1947. No match for the French military, Ho withdrew his army and government into the Viet Bac mountains in the northeast. Their first task was building support in the countryside. They recruited soldiers from the villages and drilled them in Communist ideology. Giap noted that "profound awareness of the aims of the Party, boundless loyalty to the cause of the nation and working class, and a spirit of unreserved sacrifice are fundamental questions for the army. . . . Therefore, the political work in its ranks is of first importance. *It is the soul of the army.*" [19] The Vietminh also recruited some in the civilian population to gather information about troops and equipment and to pass it on to the Vietminh.

## The Cold War Phase

The Vietminh's guerrilla tactics caused a stalemate in the war by the late 1940s. France's inability to defeat Ho's elusive army alarmed the United States and Western European nations. They were concerned that communism would spread throughout Southeast Asia, just as it had spread throughout Eastern Europe and China after World War II. The spread of communism had split the world into two opposing camps: the Communist nations led by the USSR and the non-Communist nations led by the United States. According to the popular "domino theory," Western leaders argued that if Vietnam fell to the Communists, then each Southeast Asian state would fall in a chain reaction until the entire region was under Communist control.

Seizing the opportunity to gain an ally in this Cold War rivalry, China and the Soviet Union recognized Ho's government in 1950. The United States countered by recognizing Bao Dai's government in Saigon. The French colonial government in the south was able to remain in control with help from the Vietnamese middle and upper classes in the south, royalists who backed Bao Dai, the Hoa Hao and Cao Dai religious sects, more than a million Roman Catholics, and many VNQDD and DMH members. To give the impression that it was granting self-government to its colonies, France declared the southern portion of Vietnam an independent state within the French Union in 1949, calling it the Associated States of Vietnam. Bao Dai was appointed chief of state, but France retained control of the army and foreign affairs.

In the meantime, with Chinese aid, General Giap expanded the PLA (renamed the People's Army of Vietnam, or PAVN) from 32 battalions in 1948 to 117 battalions in 1951. In 1950 the PAVN was strong enough to kill nearly six thousand French troops in battle and secure the border with China. Giap then struck the French forces in Dong Khe, Caobang province, in October 1950. The results were what historian Cecil B. Currey calls the "greatest single defeat yet suffered [before Dien Bien Phu] by the French in the history of their colonial empire." The Vietnamese captured enough equipment to supply a division, Currey writes, including "thirteen artillery pieces, 125 mortars, three platoons of tanks, 450 trucks, 940 machine guns, 1,200 submachine guns, and over 8,000 rifles."[20]

Giap continued his attacks with three separate thrusts toward Hanoi in 1951. This time he lost nearly twenty thousand troops before retreating. In early 1952 he lost another nine thousand troops in a battle along the Red River. These losses forced Giap to change his strategy to a series of smaller attacks on French outposts that isolated the French positions from each other.

## Dien Bien Phu

In 1953 Giap shifted his attention to northwest Vietnam along the Laotian border. The French had a large base in the village of Dien Bien Phu, situated in a small river valley. French commander General Henri Navarre intended to close down Vietminh supply routes out of Laos and prevent a Communist takeover of that country. Navarre also believed he could destroy Giap's northern army in one major battle.

Giap's attack on Dien Bien Phu was a bold attempt to gain the advantage in the long struggle with the French. After an interview with Giap in 1959, Hungarian diplomat Janos Radvanyi wrote, "Dien Bien Phu . . . was the last desperate exertion of the Viet Minh army. Its forces were on the verge of complete exhaustion. The supply of rice was running out. Apathy had spread among the populace to such an extent that it was difficult to draft new fighters. Years of warfare had sent morale in the fighting units to the depths."[21]

Navarre believed the Vietminh were incapable of moving heavy artillery pieces into the mountains around Dien Bien Phu and were too incompetent to use any that were already there. But he was wrong. Coolies with bicycles, donkeys, sampans, bamboo rafts, and strong backs traveled hundreds of miles of mountain roads, hacked through jungles, and climbed cliffs hauling dismantled artillery pieces and other supplies into position. With two hundred reassembled howitzers, Giap destroyed the French airstrip at Dien

*Vietnamese soldiers prepare to attack Dien Bien Phu. French and Vietnamese forces fought a fierce battle there in 1954.*

Bien Phu, making it almost impossible to land aircraft to resupply and evacuate French troops. Most of the French casualties resulted from artillery fire.

Giap's troops began their attack of the French garrison on March 13, 1954. After fifty-five days of close combat and nearly eight thousand Vietminh and twenty-two hundred French troop casualties, the last guns flared at Dien Bien Phu on May 7, 1954.

## The Geneva Agreement

On the same day that the battle of Dien Bien Phu ended, delegates from the DRVN, France, Great Britain, the Soviet Union, the Associated States of Vietnam (the Republic of Vietnam), the United States, China, Laos, and Cambodia were meeting in Geneva, Switzerland, to settle Cold War issues about Korea and Indochina.

At Geneva the DRVN sought recognition for Vietnam as an independent, unified nation. Bao Dai's Saigon government had little bargaining power, so it depended on France and the United States to secure a united, non-Communist Vietnam. China, afraid that the United States would step in and control Indochina, preferred the creation of two smaller Vietnams, with France remaining in the south and Ho Chi Minh's Communist Party in control in the north. The Americans were concerned that China would transfer troops from Korea to Vietnam in an effort to spread communism.

The final agreement set up a schedule for a cease-fire in Vietnam and temporarily divided the country at the seventeenth parallel, which would be a demilitarized zone (DMZ) with no troops permitted, and called for elections under international supervision in 1956. The agreement also allowed some French to remain in the south until the elections.

No one was satisfied with the terms. The new head of the Saigon government, Ngo Dinh Diem, rejected the agreement outright, predicting it would lead to a more deadly war in the future. The United States never signed the agreement, although the Americans promised to abide by the terms as long as no new fighting broke out and elections were held according to United Nations (UN) guidelines. Ho Chi Minh was unhappy about the partition of Vietnam, but he accepted the terms because he was confident that the Communists would be able to win nationwide elections in 1956 and unify Vietnam.

Vietnam was now officially divided into a Communist nation in the north, with 12 million people, and a non-Communist nation in the south, with 9.5 million people. Both sides agreed to allow safe evacuation of any Vietnamese who were unhappy under their new governments. More than 820,000, most of them Roman Catholics, left the north and moved into the Central Highlands and Saigon. Approximately 80,000 Vietminh soldiers and their families moved to the north.

After a decade of fighting the French, Ho Chi Minh had accomplished only partial victory. Vietnam remained divided because of the Cold War. To the non-Communist Western world, North Vietnam's government epitomized repressive communism. But to the Communist world, North Vietnam stood for liberation from capitalist exploitation by colonial powers. Both the northern and southern leaders claimed the right to govern an independent and unified Vietnam. Only a new Indo-Chinese war, this time involving the direct military action of the United States, would settle the issue.

# The Communists Unite Vietnam 3

By the time of France's defeat in 1954, the United States had already given France $2.6 billion to fight communism. When the French withdrew from Vietnam, the Americans took over the fight against the Vietminh. They supported a staunch anti-Communist, Ngo Dinh Diem, as the head of South Vietnam. However, Diem's authoritarian methods of control in the south offended the majority of the people.

The war between the north and the south heated up during the early 1960s when the United States intensified its participation in the conflict. By the late 1960s more than 540,000 American troops were fighting the Communists. Ultimately, the United States failed in its mission to defeat communism in Vietnam, and the Communist government unified the country under a single Vietnamese government for the first time in more than a hundred years.

## Diem's Rise to Power

In 1949 the French had pretended to support "independence" in Vietnam by sponsoring a government in South Vietnam with Bao Dai as emperor. However, the French retained control of the south's military, economy, and foreign affairs. After the French defeat, the United States stepped in immediately to control events in the south. American advisers considered Bao Dai a remnant of French colonialism, so in 1954 they convinced Bao Dai to offer Diem the premiership, the top position in the government. Diem demanded and got dictatorial control over the country. What he faced, however, was a country controlled by private organizations that represented organized crime, religions, Communists, and other segments of society.

The organized crime syndicate Binh Xuyen controlled the opium trade, prostitution, and gambling casinos in much of South Vietnam. Areas northwest of Saigon were ruled by a religious organization called the Cao Dai, with 2 million followers and an army of about twenty-thousand troops who supported Bao Dai. Much of the delta southwest of Saigon was dominated by the Hoa Hao, a popular Buddhist group with 1.5 million believers and an army of fifteen thousand troops.

General Edward G. Lansdale, head of the U.S. Saigon Military Mission, a covert Central Intelligence Agency (CIA) operation, helped Diem neutralize his opposition with $8 million. Diem bought the loyalty of the Cao Dai and Hoa Hao leaders and allowed their troops to join his army. With the religious sects appeased, Diem's troops were able to drive the Binh Xuyen out of Saigon in 1955.

*In 1955 Ngo Dinh Diem (foreground) took control of southern Vietnam.*

Diem's next step was to remove Emperor Bao Dai from the political scene. Because of his dictatorial powers, Diem forced the government to agree on an October 1955 referendum on whether to retain the monarchy, which would keep Bao Dai in power, or establish a republican government with Diem as president. Diem won overwhelmingly. The southern half of Vietnam officially became the Republic of Vietnam (RVN).

## A Family Affair

To govern South Vietnam, Diem chose members of his extended family to hold important government positions, much in the manner of ancient emperors. As his closest adviser and head of the secret police, Diem named a younger brother, Ngo Dinh Nhu, described by historian Cecil B. Currey as "an opium-smoking megalomaniac."[22] Nhu's wife, known as Madame Nhu, was a deputy in the RVN's National Assembly, where she promoted morality bills that outlawed singing, playing sentimental songs, and dancing in both public and private.

To promote his program, Diem created the Can Lao, or Revolutionary Personalist Workers' Party. Because Diem believed that only authoritarian governments could lead underdeveloped nations into the modern world, the Can Lao was undemocratic and tightly controlled by Nhu, Diem's brother. As historian Bernard B. Fall explains, the Can Lao imitated "Communist totalitarian methods . . . with its secret membership and five-man cells whose members knew only each other, and 'action groups' that could swiftly and quietly do away with bothersome oppositionists. Its cells existed not only throughout the government structure but also in the Vietnamese Army."[23]

## Diem's System of Control

Diem attacked his enemies relentlessly, usually labeling anyone who opposed him as a Communist. Many of the victims of his purges had no connection to communism, however. He also constructed "political reeducation centers," where he imprisoned tens of thousands of people who disagreed with him. Scholar P.J. Honey investigated these centers in 1959 and concluded that "the consensus of the opinion expressed by these peoples [in the camps] is that . . . the majority of the detainees are neither communists nor pro-Communists."[24]

By the late 1950s, Diem seemed firmly in control. Even the Vietnamese Workers' Party (formerly the ICP in North Vietnam) admitted that between 1954 and 1960 Diem had remarkable success in stabilizing conditions in the south. Diem's government controlled families with the house-block system. Historian William J. Duiker explains that this system was a " Saigon-run security network in which families throughout the RVN were organized into units of five and made jointly responsible for the loyalty of all their members."[25]

## Insurgency in the South

Diem's control of South Vietnam was limited, however. Several thousand Communists had remained in the south rather than move to North Vietnam after the 1954 Geneva Agreement. Diem called them Viet Nam Cong San (Vietcong), or Vietnamese Communists. The Vietcong spent the next five years organizing and preparing people to oppose the Diem regime.

At first the Vietcong generally operated independently from Ho's Communist government in Hanoi. However, in 1959 the Communist Party in the north detected an increase in anti-Diem sentiment and therefore encouraged the Vietcong to increase its insurgency in the south. The Vietcong began infiltrating village and worker organizations, overthrowing local leaders, and creating new village governments. They established "liberated zones" in the Mekong Delta and the Central Highlands. The Central Office of South Vietnam (COSVN), a Communist front organization disbanded in 1954, was revived to coordinate the rebellion in the south. In December 1960 the Hanoi leaders sponsored the formation in the south of the National Front for the Liberation of South Vietnam (NLF), which combined the Vietcong and non-Communists who opposed Diem into a single revolutionary party.

## Problems with the Economy

Diem faced several obstacles in trying to modernize South Vietnam's economy. When France withdrew its military and colonial government, more than 150,000 Vietnamese lost their jobs, and many of them remained unemployed. Almost 900,000 refugees from North Vietnam added to this mass of unemployed. In addition the only industries in the south in 1955 were small. These industries included the production of soft drinks, industrial gases, cigarettes, and matches. Diem's government attracted very little foreign investment, so it had almost no money to build large industrial projects. Out of a workforce of 4 million, only about 50,000 workers held jobs in industry. The rest of the southerners worked in agriculture.

The vast majority of southerners owned very tiny plots or were tenant farmers. The majority of farming land was owned by only a few thousand rich landlords. To gain the support of the peasants, Diem introduced a series of land-reform programs that changed the peasants' conditions very little. As the U.S. Department of State reported:

> As of 1960, 45% of the land remained concentrated in the hands of 2% of landowners, and 15% of the landlords owned 75% of all the land. Those relatively few farmers who did benefit from the [land-reform] program were more often than not northerners, refugees, Catholics, or Annamese—so that land reform added to the GVN's [Government of Vietnam's] aura of favoritism which deepened peasant alienation in Cochinchina. [26]

One problem with Diem's land-reform programs was the people he appointed to administer the programs. They were mostly rich landowners and officials close to Diem who conspired with each other to profit from land reform. They offered high-interest loans to peasants to buy land that many of them had farmed for decades. In addition, since many peasants were already in debt because of high rents and taxes, they could not borrow more money to buy their land.

## The Strategic Hamlet Program

Land reform in South Vietnam failed also because the programs were primarily devised to fight Communists rather than to improve people's economic circumstances. Often, the reform required that people relocate, and peasants resented being moved away from their home villages to start all over again. The strategic hamlet program, proposed by U.S. president John F. Kennedy and directed by Diem's brother Ngo Dinh Nhu, is a good example of the misguided policy of land reform. The United States and South Vietnam planned to "pacify" the Mekong Delta by creating eleven thousand strategic hamlets that would be protected from Vietcong attack. Inhabitants built fences, moats, and other defense devices around their villages. If the Vietcong came, villagers were supposed to deny them food and information. But as historian Stanley Karnow writes, "The program often converted peasants into Vietcong sympathizers. Peasants in many places resented working without pay . . . against an enemy that did not threaten them but directed its sights against government officials."[27]

On October 1, 1962, Diem reported that "the population living in safety and revolution inside the strategic hamlets already built (3,074) or about to be completed (2,679), numbers 7,267,517 souls."[28] What Diem, Nhu, and the U.S. officials did not know was that the Vietcong had infiltrated Diem's government so extensively that Nhu had unknowingly appointed one as head administrator of the strategic hamlet program. Colonel Pham Ngoc Thao, a Vietcong spy in the Army of the Republic of Vietnam, knew that the program would alienate the villagers, so he enthusiastically promoted it. The program was such a dismal failure that a year after its launch in Binh-Duong province, north of Saigon, the Vietcong took back control of the pilot villages.

## The November 1963 Coup

During his nine years of rule, Diem was perceived as an elitist who headed a corrupt government. But Diem's fall from power was accelerated in 1963 because of his administration's attempts to suppress Buddhists. On May 8, tens of thousands of Buddhists gathered in cities to celebrate Buddha's 2,527th birthday. The government prohibited them from flying Buddhist flags during the celebration. When they defied the government, another of Diem's brothers sent troops to break up the huge crowds in Hue. Nine people were killed and several were injured. Buddhists across the

*Police clash with Buddhist demonstrators during the 1963 protests that precipitated Ngo Dinh Diem's fall from power.*

country protested. Then, in June, a sixty-six-year-old Buddhist monk immolated himself to protest Diem's anti-Buddhist actions, and Associated Press photographs of the event shocked the world.

Alarmed by the extensive opposition to Diem, President Kennedy sent a new ambassador to Saigon, Henry David Lodge, to assess the situation. Lodge learned that a group of rebel generals had planned a coup, but they wanted word that the United States would back them. In a cable to Kennedy on August 29, Lodge wrote, "We are launched on a course from which there is no respectable turning back: the overthrow of the Diem government. . . . There is no turning back because there is no possibility, in my view, that the war can be won under a Diem administration." Kennedy responded, "While we do not wish to stimulate a coup, we also do not wish to leave the impression that the United States would thwart a change of government." [29]

With American backing, the rebel generals arrested Diem and Nhu on November 1. But instead of putting them on trial, as the Americans had expected, the generals assassinated the brothers. After the public was told that Diem and Nhu had committed suicide, the people celebrated in the streets. A military revolutionary council consisting of twelve men chaired by General Duong Van Minh took over the government.

## America's Reputation Is at Stake

President Kennedy worried that Americans would no longer support aid to Vietnam after Diem's fall. He knew that Saigon's government still needed help to defeat the Communists. He decided that the United States would expand its training and advising of the South Vietnamese army. To do this, Kennedy increased the number of military advisers involved in the Military Assistance Command, Vietnam (MACV), program from about 750 in 1961 to nearly 20,000 by the fall of 1963. To Kennedy and most American leaders, the U.S. reputation as the defender of the "free world" was at stake.

When Kennedy was assassinated in November 1963, Lyndon Johnson took over the presidency. Although fully aware of American support for the South Vietnamese, President Johnson felt trapped by the fighting. The conflict in Vietnam diverted his energy away from a long list of economic reforms he had planned for the American society. But he realized he needed to champion the war, stating that if he let the Communists take over South Vietnam, "I would be seen as a coward and my nation would be seen as an appeaser, and we would both find it impossible to accomplish anything for anybody anywhere on the entire globe." [30]

## The Gulf of Tonkin Incident

The event that provoked American leaders to send combat troops to Vietnam came in 1964. On July 30 and August 1, CIA-trained South Vietnamese commandos raided northern installations in the Gulf of Tonkin. The Hanoi government retaliated on August 2 by sending torpedo boats to attack the U.S. destroyer *Maddox,* a ship equipped to record enemy radar and radio transmissions. It failed to deter the *Maddox,* and with the assistance of U.S. jets from the aircraft carrier *Ticonderoga,* the Americans sunk one North Vietnamese torpedo boat and crippled two more.

More attacks on the *Maddox* followed during the day of August 4, and in the evening the crew interpreted radar activity as another enemy attack. The two destroyers began firing, and jets from the *Ticonderoga* circled the ships looking for attack boats. The sonar crews reported that twenty-two torpedoes had been fired at them, and the ships reported two or three North Vietnamese boats sunk. However, *Maddox* commander Captain John Herrick was never convinced they had been attacked. He later testified that all the enemy activity could have been false readings from radar gone crazy from "freak weather effects." [31]

Without waiting for an investigation, Johnson ordered the first bombing mission over Vietnam on August 4. Sixty-four sorties damaged several patrol boat bases and an oil storage depot. Two U.S. jets were shot down, and one pilot, Lieutenant Everett Alvarez Jr., ejected over North Vietnam. He was the first of almost six hundred American airmen to serve time as a prisoner of war (POW).

The next day Johnson submitted to Congress the Gulf of Tonkin Resolution. It passed unanimously in the House of Representatives and with only two negative votes in the Senate. The resolution authorized the president "to take all necessary measures to repel any armed attack against the forces of the United States and to prevent further aggression" and to use force "to assist any member or protocol state of the Southeast Asia Collective Defense Treaty requesting assistance in defense of its freedom." [32]

## The American Buildup

Within months of the Gulf of Tonkin incident, the first U.S. combat troops were sent to Vietnam. The increase of troops followed shortly after the Vietcong killed fifty Americans in February 1965. Johnson retaliated with bombing attacks. Then, in March, he sent two U.S. Marine combat battalions (3,500 troops) to defend Da Nang Air Base, where American bombers were stationed. Another

*President Lyndon Johnson visits U.S. soldiers stationed in Vietnam. Johnson sent the first combat troops to the country in 1964.*

70,000 U.S. Marines and Army troops followed soon after to defend American bases. Within a year of the Gulf of Tonkin Resolution, 180,000 U.S. soldiers were in Vietnam under the command of General William Westmoreland. Troop numbers expanded rapidly, until about 540,000 American soldiers were serving in Vietnam by the end of 1968.

Johnson expected that bombing would pressure North Vietnam to negotiate for peace. Instead, the government in Hanoi disassembled whole industries and moved them to remote mountain locations. In South Vietnam the Vietcong intensified their activity, recruiting youths, women, peasants, and others dissatisfied with the South Vietnamese government.

## General Nguyen Van Thieu

While increasing troop strength in Vietnam, American advisers were trying to convince the South Vietnamese government to find a way to compromise with the north. In June 1965 Air Vice Marshal Nguyen Cao Ky and General Nguyen Van Thieu took over the South Vietnamese government after a military coup. Although competitors for power, they were convinced in 1967 to run as a team in an election for president (Thieu) and vice president (Ky). They won easily, but Thieu opposed any compromise with North Vietnam. When the United States threatened to withdraw aid, Thieu sent representatives to Paris, where informal peace talks had begun in 1968.

Although Thieu's main concern was fighting the war, he did institute a few reforms. In villages under his control, elections were held and land grants were given to people who actually worked the land. But the pressure from the Americans to "Vietnamize" the war (turn all the fighting over to South Vietnamese troops) put Thieu in a political bind. Whatever he did to raise money for defense and troops for the army antagonized large segments of South Vietnam. Although Thieu won a second term as president in 1971, many considered the election fraudulent because most of Thieu's competitors had been disqualified, including Ky.

## The Communists' Strategy

The military coup in South Vietnam in 1965 suggested to the Communist leadership that it might be time to begin a more aggressive phase of fighting. Led by party secretary Le Duan, the Communists initiated the "southern strategy," which channeled more troops from the People's Army of Vietnam (PAVN) into the south to face the American and South Vietnamese armies in conventional battles. General Giap's units suffered enormous casualties as a result. In his first major confrontation with American troops, the battle for Ia Drang Valley in November 1965, he withdrew after more than two thousand of his troops were killed.

Although unhappy with the high casualty rate, the Communist leadership believed that the southern government had little popular support. Therefore, in April 1967 North Vietnam decided to launch a larger offensive in the south, expecting it to trigger a "spontaneous uprising" and enable the north "to win a decisive victory in the shortest possible time."[33] In July 1967 the PAVN commander died, and Giap was once again in charge of North Vietnam's military operations. He still preferred guerrilla war, but he obeyed the party's instructions to prepare a big offensive against South Vietnam for the Tet (Chinese New Year) holiday beginning on January 30, 1968.

## The Tet Offensive

Giap began the Tet Offensive by attacking Khe Sanh, an American base near the Laotian border in Quang Tri province and other bases near the DMZ. U.S. general Westmoreland sent half of his troops to defend Khe Sanh, convinced Giap would avoid attacking large population centers in South Vietnam.

The attacks on Khe Sanh and other border bases, although costly in casualties to Giap, were diversionary operations. With his main force of eighty-four thousand NLF and PAVN troops,

*A North Vietnamese woman mourns her husband, killed in the Tet Offensive. Communist forces suffered very heavy casualties during the offensive.*

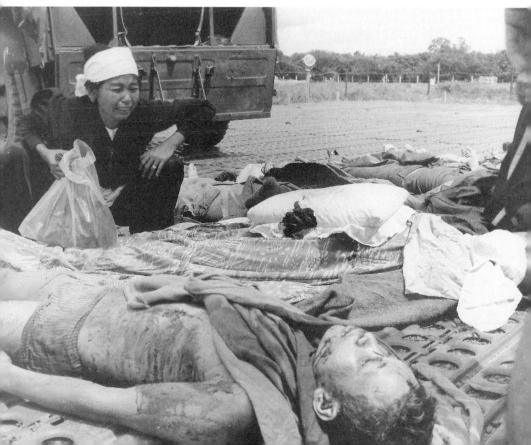

Giap attacked forty-one of the forty-four southern provincial capitals and five of the major cities, including Saigon and Hue, on the early mornings of January 30 and 31, 1968. U.S. and ARVN troops fought back and claimed victory after two months of fighting when Giap withdrew his forces. He suffered massive losses: forty thousand dead compared to only eleven hundred American and twenty-three hundred South Vietnamese killed. A million southerners became homeless because of the fighting, and the Vietcong's ability to carry on the war was greatly reduced. From this point on, the North Vietnamese government began sending more of its own forces to fight in the south. No match for superior American military technology, however, the north returned to Giap's principles of guerrilla fighting.

Although a disaster on the battlefield, Tet proved to be a major political victory for North Vietnam. The fighting made daily headlines in the United States, and Americans began to turn against the war. When General Westmoreland asked for an additional 206,000 combat troops, President Johnson refused and replaced him with General Creighton Abrams. Johnson also reduced the bombing, hoping to convince North Vietnam that the United States would compromise at the peace talks in Paris.

## The Ho Chi Minh Trail

In 1959 the North Vietnamese leaders decided to create a military supply route through the Truong Son mountains along western Vietnam that would pass through Laos and Cambodia into South Vietnam northwest of Saigon.

Americans knew the Truong Son Trail as the Ho Chi Minh Trail. Extending more than 620 miles north to south, the Ho Chi Minh Trail actually consisted of 12,000 miles of camouflaged roads, trails, and paths through mountains and jungle, with underground barracks and hospitals. A hundred thousand people worked along the trail as porters, mechanics, engineers, and guards. Between 1966 and 1971 more than six hundred thousand North Vietnamese soldiers entered the south along the trail. In addition, North Vietnam channeled much of its military supplies through the Ho Chi Minh Trail.

# The Vietnamization of the War

President Richard Nixon based his campaign platform on the premise that the war must be won by South Vietnamese troops, referred to as the "Vietnamization" of the war. He promised to withdraw all American combat troops during his administration. Within a year of taking office, Nixon reduced U.S. troop strength from 545,000 to 430,000, and by December 1970 the number had shrunk to 280,000. As the South Vietnamese army expanded to over a million soldiers, Nixon continued to withdraw U.S. forces. At the end of 1971, fewer than 175,000 American troops were in Vietnam, and only about 75,000 of them were engaged in some kind of combat.

In 1970 Nixon decided to showcase the fighting ability of the South Vietnamese army in a campaign to cut off the southern routes of the Ho Chi Minh Trail in Cambodia. This 620-mile-long trail was the major supply route for the northern army. In the Cambodian campaign, fifty thousand ARVN troops captured large caches of arms and supplies and killed several thousand Communist troops. But as soon as ARVN and U.S. support troops pulled back, the Communists returned to their bases. The operation was canceled in January 1971, without destroying the Communists' bases in Cambodia.

# Peace Negotiations

Peace talks between the North Vietnamese and the United States began in May 1968. The Saigon government joined the talks in January 1969. But no agreements came out of the meetings. Away from the formal talks, U.S. national security adviser Henry Kissinger met secretly with North Vietnamese representative Le Duc Tho from 1970 to 1972, working out terms for ending the war. Eventually, representatives of the United States, South Vietnam, North Vietnam, and the NLF signed the Paris Agreement on January 27, 1973.

The treaty called for a cease-fire, promised complete American withdrawal, allowed three hundred thousand Vietcong troops to stay in place in the south, provided for the release of all POWs, guaranteed southerners a fair and free election to determine their future government, and pledged reunification of North and South Vietnam through peaceful negotiations. Only two of the provisions were carried out: Vietcong troops stayed in place in South Vietnam, and the final U.S. combat troops left on March 29, 1973.

Thieu probably never intended to abide by the agreement. Historian Ngo Vinh Long writes that immediately after the agreement was signed, Thieu restated his "Four No's" policy, which called for "no recognition of the enemy, no coalition government, no neutralization of the southern region of Vietnam, and no concession of territory."[34] The fighting continued. Thieu claimed that he lost forty-one thousand troops in the next six months. Morale among his troops dropped to an all-time low, with almost two hundred thousand ARVN troops deserting in 1974.

## The Final Days and Surrender

The South Vietnamese economy collapsed when the Americans withdrew. Thieu's government lost the support of Buddhists and other moderate organizations. Le Duan and his northern colleagues, seeing an opening to overpower their enemy, decided on a final assault they believed would defeat South Vietnam. Giap was too sick to lead, so the Politburo appointed General Van Tien Dung to take over.

The north felt the south would lose quickly without U.S. intervention. To test American intentions, General Dung struck in Phuoc Long province, only fifty miles from Saigon. On January 6, 1975, the provincial capital fell without an American military response. Buoyed by their success, the Communists continued their march through South Vietnam. Pleiku, Hue, and Da Nang fell with little resistance. By the end of March the South Vietnamese army had collapsed and officers were fleeing for safety. The Communist Party leaders in Hanoi, thrilled by Dung's success, ordered him to take Saigon before the May rainy season. Dung named his attack the "Ho Chi Minh Campaign."

On April 21 President Thieu resigned and fled to Taiwan. On April 26 Dung began his move on Saigon with 130,000 troops. They met resistance, but by April 30 all ARVN troops had surrendered. Thirty years after the opening shots of their war against the French, the Vietnamese Communists had finally unified their nation and changed the country's name to the Socialist Republic of Vietnam.

# A Shaky
# Beginning 4

The Socialist Republic of Vietnam (SRVN) was ruled by uncompromising Communist Party leaders who believed they could create a model Socialist society. However, they faced a formidable task in the south, where the people had practiced free enterprise for almost a century. The Hanoi Communist government set out to eliminate all remnants of capitalism and punish people associated with the former southern government.

The leaders' problems in nation building were complicated by wars with Cambodia and China. Vietnam could not afford to demobilize its military and concentrate on economic development because of the hostilities posed by those countries.

## Transforming the South

Immediately after their victory in the south, the Communist Party began restructuring southern society so that the people would abandon their capitalist ideas and accept socialism. One of the party's plans was to move almost the entire 4 million citizens of Ho Chi Minh City into new economic zones located in uninhabited areas outside of the cities. The government hoped that each economic zone would become self-governing and economically self-sufficient. In the first year after the war, the party relocated 600,000 people to economic zones created along the Cambodian border and in the Central Highlands. From 1976 to 1981, 1.5 million people were moved into these and other newly created zones.

However, very few people moved willingly. The new economic zones became places of internal exile for Vietnamese who refused to follow the party's directives. When possible, they would escape back to the cities by bribing party officials and guards.

Another way the Communist government dealt with recalcitrant southerners was by sending them to reeducation camps. Party leaders thought the majority of southerners would change if they were isolated in camps and given lessons in communism. About eighty camps were located mostly in remote jungles and mountains, so prisoners could not escape. Those sent to the camps included almost all former officers of ARVN, civil servants of the former southern government, religious leaders, teachers, writers, scientists, and other intellectuals. Historian Kelly Evans-Pfeifer describes their treatment in the camps: "[They] were forced to dig canals, build dams, clear jungles, and, in a few cases, build more camps. . . . The reeducation process involved lectures and readings on American imperialism, Vietnamese nationalism, and socialism. Prisoners were forced to write regular reports detailing their 'crimes.'" [35]

Approximately a million southerners were confined in the camps for periods ranging from a few months to several years. There were approximately 120,000 people living in reeducation camps in the early 1980s before the government began moderating its policy. By 1985 the number of prisoners in the camps had been reduced to about 40,000.

## Refugees
Fearing Communist persecution after the war, more than 1 million South Vietnamese fled the country. About 150,000 were evacuated by the Americans in the spring of 1975 as the northern troops marched through the south. Close to 560,000 "boat people" escaped the authorities by slipping away on small boats and fishing vessels. The remaining ones left Vietnam through various refugee programs, such as the U.S. Orderly Departure Program and the U.S. asylum program for political prisoners and Asian American children.

Most commonly, only one or two members of a family were able to escape. While drifting at sea, refugees were attacked by pirates, ran out of food and fresh water, and suffered from diseases. Many thousands died before being rescued by passing ships. Survivors were placed in refugee camps in Southeast Asian nations such as Thailand, the Philippines, Hong Kong, Malaysia, and Indonesia. Usually, several thousand refugees stayed in these camps for many months, living in makeshift housing while church groups and the United Nations sought nations that would offer them sanctuary.

*Fearing Communist persecution after the war, more than 1 million refugees like these fled South Vietnam.*

In addition to the almost 600,000 refugees who settled in the United States, another 150,000 settled in Australia. About 280,000 ethnic Chinese (Hoa) from Vietnam went to live in China. About 215,000 refugees lived in temporary camps in Hong Kong before they could be resettled elsewhere; about 1,500 were allowed to stay in Hong Kong permanently. Tens of thousands of refugees in Hong Kong returned to Vietnam in the 1990s.

## Creating a Socialist Society

The majority of people in the south stayed and reluctantly adapted to the new Communist ideology being imposed by the government. Communists teach that selfishness and greed drive capitalism, so those who perpetuate the capitalism must change their views. The result will be a compassionate society with workers dedicated to the welfare of the society.

After 1954 Communists in the north began a program to eliminate landlords, rich farmers, and business owners. Almost everyone who owned more than two acres lost their land in this land-reform program. Tens of thousands of these victims were upright citizens who had fought bravely for independence and contributed to the prosperity of their communities. Many were Roman Catholics, Buddhists, and members of non-Communist groups who had fought with the Vietminh against the French.

Landowners who had cooperated with the French usually received the death penalty. By 1958 approximately fifty thousand landlords had been executed. Even rich peasants, those with more than three acres of land who hired seasonal workers, lost their land. As the confiscations, tortures, and deaths spread, the people became restless and started demonstrating for a halt of the program. Ho Chi Minh ordered the military to quell the dissenters. In Nghe An province alone, nearly six thousand people were executed in 1956 for protesting. However, Ho Chi Minh became alarmed by the discontent throughout the country and stopped the program, warning that "it cannot be said of a group of people that they are all good or bad."[36] Ho admitted publicly that the party had made mistakes in carrying out land reform.

## Cooperatives

The Communists' land-reform policy worked for a while, however. The Communists redistributed confiscated land to approximately 2 million landless peasant families, but their ownership of the land was short-lived. In the late 1950s the government began a campaign to organize peasants into cooperatives. Under this economic system, plots, draft animals, and tools were collected under the direction of party leadership. Farmers were then required to deposit their harvest with the cooperative officials. Peasants were repaid with ration booklets with which to buy food and supplies. By 1963 almost 88 percent of rural families in the north worked for cooperatives.

The party converted almost all enterprises—from factories to handicraft shops—into cooperatives, resulting in the government owning almost all the means of production. The Communist Party then appointed party members as political advisers to every workplace, whether a cement plant or a vegetable cooperative. These advisers worked side by side with managers to ensure that party policies, from production to distribution of products, were followed. The cooperative system made it easier for the party to control peasants' lives.

*A young Vietnamese boy lies in front of a propagandist mural highlighting the benefits of Communist cooperatives.*

## Monitoring People's Lives

To ensure that the people conformed to party policies, the Communist leaders expanded the traditional Vietnamese custom of the government monitoring the everyday lives of citizens. Before the French ruled, the Vietnamese had been required to register in villages and get official approval to move around. When the French took over, they required that each Vietnamese adult carry an identity card. The Communist Party established the *ho khau* system, or household registration, which required each household to have a registration card. This card enabled citizens to receive housing, buy supplies from the state-run stores, collect state subsidies of food, and travel. People living away from their home without government permission were unable to acquire a registration card. Without the card, they were unable to obtain any assistance from the government.

The party established People's Committees in every neighborhood and commune. Party members were assigned to these committees to instruct and guide the residents and workers in proper Socialist principles. Until the 1990s, the party required families to meet almost weekly to discuss Marxist-Leninist guidelines for behavior.

When the war with the United States ended, the National Assembly assigned to the local Public Security Forces the usual law enforcement duties of arresting and detaining suspects, searching homes, and issuing and checking ID cards and other documents. However, an even more effective organization that served to control social behavior was the Revolutionary Vigilance Committees (RVCs). According to historian Douglas Pike, these RVCs existed on almost every city block as well as at most workplaces. As Pike describes, each was "headed by a warden and made up of a team of neighbors, usually 25 to 40 households (120 to 300 persons). . . . Its purpose was to 'help the government in all ways and aspects,' specifically by monitoring the behavior of its members, reporting public opinion to higher authorities, and promoting various state and party policies and programs locally." [37]

Another effective control device is the *ly lich,* an official file on each person compiled by the Communist Party and kept by the Ministry of the Interior. Information about each person, from family background and religious practice to work attitude and conversations about the party, is recorded. Until the late 1990s, the party gave people from peasant and worker families priority for school admittance, job selection, and other privileges in society.

Also until the late 1990s, the party required people who wanted to travel away from their home villages to carry written permission from their employer. Before they could leave the village, the local police office had to add its approval. Upon reaching their destination, travelers had to acquire another stamp of approval from that police office. When they returned home, travelers had to check in again with the home police. This kind of bureaucratic red tape was routine, so many people resorted to bribing officials to gain privileges.

## Economic Disaster

Southerners tended to resist these heavy-handed methods of social control. However, the Fourth National (Communist) Party Congress, which met in December 1976, was determined to force

---

## The Cost of the War to Vietnam

The cost of the war with America was enormous. Estimates of casualties vary, but civilian and military casualties in both the north and the south totaled more than 4 million people, more than 10 percent of the population. The number of wounded easily exceeded 10 million. Another million or more South Vietnamese fled their country, afraid of possible Communist retributions. Those escaping included many well-educated and skilled professionals and workers who could have helped a free Vietnam rebound after the war.

The war also wrecked Vietnam's economy. Normal businesses and industrial production were constantly interrupted by U.S. bombing. Workers in the north spent most of their time repairing roads and buildings.

southerners to accept socialism. The party declared that industry and agriculture in the south would come under state control within three years. In its attempt to eradicate capitalism, the party closed hundreds of thousands of private businesses between 1975 and 1980.

By 1980 Vietnam's economy was in a shambles. An estimated 20 percent of nonagricultural workers were unemployed. The average per capita income in the nation hovered around two hundred U.S. dollars. Peasants were even worse off; because of bad climate, poor management, and a lack of supplies, they were not even growing enough food for themselves. As a result, the country was suffering from chronic food shortages. More than 25 percent of the people under fifteen years of age were suffering from malnutrition.

Southerners continued to resist the Communist Party's plans. According to historian Ronald J. Cima, by 1985 "only 66 percent of cultivated land and 72 percent of peasant households in the South had been organized into collectivized production . . . , and socialist transformation in private industry had led to decreased production, increased production costs, and decreased product quality."[38]

Many southerners who had supported the fight against American and South Vietnamese forces had turned against the Communist government by 1985. Scholars Doan Van Toai and David Chanoff describe them as "unhappy about the rigid, Soviet-style approach to economic planning that has resulted in industrial and agricultural stagnation, and about the 'class struggle' social policies that have imprisoned or ostracized many of the South's most competent administrators and technocrats."[39]

## Free Enterprise

Party general secretary Le Duan and his supporters realized they needed to make adjustments to their economic plans. They already had allowed private businesses to reopen in Ho Chi Minh City before 1979. At the Fifth Party Congress in 1982, party officials discontinued their plan to nationalize all small enterprises. Southerners were allowed to operate their own small businesses, as they had before the war.

To stimulate agriculture, the party decided to try a mixture of capitalist and Socialist techniques. They called their plan "family economy." This system allowed households to make a contract with the cooperative officials to farm a specific plot of government land. Each household had to produce a certain amount to pay the officials for rent and taxes. Households could then sell any surplus crops either on the free market or to the government for a fixed price. Peasants responded positively to the family economy program.

For Vietnam to become a strong, self-supporting nation, however, it needed to speed industrial development. The government had hoped to make a profit from increased agricultural production to reinvest in building up industry. However, by 1986 Vietnamese agriculture had not grown fast enough to support new industry.

## The Cambodian Problem

Besides a ruined economy, Vietnam's road to nation building was complicated by wars with its neighbors. In the early 1970s North Vietnam had supported the army of the Communist Party of Kampuchea (CPK) led by Pol Pot. In 1975 the CPK defeated an American-supported army under General Lon Nol. However, Pol Pot harbored a deep hate of all Vietnamese. He was determined that Cambodia, which he named the Democratic Republic of Kampuchea, would be free of Vietnamese influence.

Vietnamese Communists had trained about five thousand CPK members and expected them to keep close links with Vietnam. However, Pol Pot had them all killed because of their ties to Vietnam. In early 1975 the Khmer Rouge (Khmer Communists) attacked Vietnam's troops on islands in the Gulf of Thailand. Pol Pot then began a campaign to kill all Vietnamese living in Cambodia.

Pol Pot's intentions were clear. He told a radio audience, "Until now, we have attained our goal: Thirty dead Vietnamese for every single Cambodian. We could sacrifice two million Cambodians to exterminate the fifty million Vietnamese—and [we] would still be six million."[40] According to scholar Ben Kiernan, Pol Pot's targets were not just the Vietnamese but also the 1.5 million "Khmer bodies with Vietnamese minds"[41] who lived in eastern Cambodia.

*The Khmer Rouge killed more than 1 million people under Pol Pot. Remains of some of the victims fill this Cambodian museum exhibit.*

Under Pol Pot's orders, more than 1 million Khmers were killed, in addition to at least 8,000 Vietnamese, 200,000 Chinese, 100,000 Muslims, and 20,000 Thais living inside of Cambodia.

## The Vietnamese-Cambodian War

Determined to end Pol Pot's reign of terror, the Vietnamese government sent ninety thousand troops into Cambodia in late 1977. The Khmer Rouge battled them to a stalemate. Finally, on Christmas Day 1978, the Vietnamese leaders attacked with several divisions. Within weeks, they occupied the major cities of Cambodia and set up a puppet government called the People's Republic of Kampuchea (PRK). In the countryside and forests, Pol Pot continued to resist. Vietnam lost more than fifty-five thousand soldiers in the fighting.

About 220,000 Vietnamese troops occupied Cambodia by January 1979, and they settled in for almost a decade trying to control the country. However, they were unable to subdue the Khmer Rouge. Historian Margaret Slocomb explains that the Khmer Rouge simply withdrew into mountain forests near the Thailand border and regrouped. They continued guerrilla attacks for almost a decade, but they never were strong enough to defeat the Vietnamese.

During the war, Vietnam wanted to join the Association of Southeast Asian Nations (ASEAN) to get help for its economy. ASEAN would only accept Vietnam as a member if it would allow a coalition of Cambodian political groups to run Cambodia. In June 1982 Vietnam permitted Cambodia, then called Democratic Kampuchea, to form a new government; however, Vietnamese troops remained in the country to fight Pol Pot and his Khmer Rouge, who continued their guerrilla resistance. By the late 1980s Vietnam decided to shift its energy to solving economic problems at home and began withdrawing its troops. The last Vietnamese troops left Cambodia in 1989.

## The Vietnamese-Chinese War

The Vietnamese-Cambodian war alarmed Chinese leaders, who were competing with the USSR for influence in the Communist world. Both China and the USSR sought to gain allies in Southeast Asia. In 1978 Vietnam and the USSR signed the Treaty of Friendship and Cooperation, which gave the Soviets use of Vietnam's Cam Ranh Bay military base in exchange for Russian military and economic aid. However, China had always considered mainland Southeast Asia as its own domain. With Soviet help, China feared, Vietnam might be able to challenge its power in the region. Therefore, China threw its support behind Pol Pot and the Khmer Rouge.

Territorial claims also added to the tension between Vietnam and China. The two nations had fought for centuries over land along their 740-mile border. Both also claimed ownership of the Paracel and Spratly Islands in the South China Sea.

Complicating their strained relations was Vietnam's harsh treatment of its Chinese residents, the Hoa. Living in separate communities, the Hoa had built up successful businesses and become relatively rich, especially in the south. In 1977, however, the Vietnamese government program of nationalizing businesses forced the Hoa to sell their enterprises to the government. In Ho Chi Minh

City alone, 1.5 million Hoa were forced to move into new, undeveloped economic zones in the rural areas.

In the north, Vietnamese officials began investigating and harassing the Hoa as potential enemies of the government. As conditions worsened during the mid-1970s, tens of thousands of Hoa left Vietnam. When the Vietnamese government stopped three Chinese ships from boarding Hoa passengers going to China, China threatened to retaliate. Chinese troop movements along the border increased, and Chinese planes crossed into Vietnam harassing villages in late October 1978. Finally, in February 1979, China decided to attack with combat troops. The war lasted less than month, ending on March 5 with the Chinese withdrawal from Vietnamese territory.

Both sides claimed victory, but none of the issues was settled. Violence erupted periodically along the border and at sea during the 1980s. Attempts to settle their differences continued for almost two decades. Finally, on December 30, 1999, the two nations signed a treaty that settled their common border. They also promised to continue negotiations to settle peacefully their disputes in the South China Sea.

## Vietnam's Relations with the Two Superpowers

In its wars with Cambodia and China, Vietnam had the support of the Soviet Union. Vietnam became a member of the United Nations in 1977 because of Soviet backing. The Soviets continued to provide assistance to Vietnam during the early 1980s. However, Soviet aid diminished steadily as the USSR's Communist system began collapsing during the mid-1980s.

In the long run, the key to Vietnam's economic future was normalizing relations with the United States. When the Vietnam War ended in 1975, the United States extended its trade embargo on North Vietnam to cover all of Vietnam. Over the next decade, American officials refused to discuss lifting the embargo until the Vietnamese gave a detailed accounting of Americans missing in action (MIA) from the war. Another barrier to improving relations was Vietnam's continued occupation of Cambodia during

*A Vietnamese soldier guards a Chinese prisoner during Vietnam's short war with China in 1979.*

the 1980s. When Vietnam began offering information on American MIAs and withdrew from Cambodia, the United States hinted that if Vietnam would also open its economy to free enterprise, American economic aid might follow.

## Vietnam: A Decade After Unification

The problems in Vietnam, according to Vo Van Kiet, vice chairman of the Council of Ministers, stemmed from poor planning and guidance from government agencies. A major problem, Kiet said, was the government-set prices for specific crops. Farmers grew only enough of the required crops, such as rice, corn, and sweet potatoes, to pay their rent and taxes to the government. They had no incentive to grow more because they would have to sell this surplus to the government for the fixed low prices. Instead, farmers grew cash crops that brought them higher profits because they were sold on the free market.

The economic problems also extended into industry. Because the state owned all industry, the tens of thousands of plants and factories operated inefficiently and lost money every year. The government had to print money just to pay workers' salaries and benefits. By 1986 the Communist Party leaders realized that they had failed to establish a secure and economically sound nation.

# Seeking a Place in the World 5

In December 1986 Vietnam's Communist Party (CPV) gathered in Hanoi for the Sixth National Party Congress. Their nation was in trouble economically, and the people's confidence in the party's leadership was disappearing. If it could not solve their economic woes, the party itself would be in danger of losing its control over the nation.

Many leaders were convinced that only a dramatic shift in economic philosophy would save the nation. They needed expertise and investments from Western nations to modernize Vietnam's economy. But to gain international confidence that Vietnam was worthy of receiving foreign assistance, Vietnam had to prove it was establishing a sound economic foundation for private companies and investors. By shifting to a free market economy, Vietnam encouraged normalization of economic trade with the United States.

At the congress, party secretary Nguyen Van Linh convinced the majority of party members that a reform program called *doi moi,* or "renovation," should be approved. The new program called for a mixture of government planning and free market strategies in business. Collectives were abolished, thus freeing farmers and businesses to sell products directly in the marketplace for profit. In addition, thousands of state-owned enterprises were targeted for privatization, forcing them to compete with other private businesses.

## Consensus Politics

Linh succeeded in getting *doi moi* approved, even though behind the scenes party members were split over policy. The disastrous failure of the economy during the 1980s brought these differences to the surface.

One group within the party still call themselves Communists, but they are essentially pragmatists. They see themselves as guiding Vietnam into the future using economic ideas that have proven successful in other countries. Therefore, they encourage private enterprise and competition to build up industry and agriculture. At the opposite extreme are the traditionalists; these are hard-line Communists who argue that capitalist methods will divide the nation and lead to widespread exploitation by the rich.

Most party leaders find themselves supporting positions in between these extremes. They understand that Vietnam will not survive under hard-line communism, but they want to preserve the Communist Party's control over the nation. By seeking compromises that will promote slow, steady change, these centrists also believe they can preserve the party's political control over the nation. This tendency to seek consensus has characterized Vietnamese politics over the decades. When hard-liner Do Muoi became general secretary of the party in 1991, people anticipated restraints on free market reforms. Instead, he negotiated with the pragmatists to ensure strong, steady economic growth.

In addition to these three political groupings, many different interest groups influence political decisions. Among these are organizations that speak for labor, women, youth, minorities, provinces, and individual cities. Scholar David Koh explains, "A leader who wants a smooth term would find it difficult to press for radical and quick changes and would want to avoid stepping on too many toes. This is an important dynamic in the leadership selection process."[42] As a result, decisions in Vietnamese politics are made only after long negotiations that aim for compromise and consensus. It is impossible for one person to dominate Vietnamese politics.

Today, the power in Vietnam resides with the persons in three top positions. This trio includes Communist Party secretary Nong Duc Manh, Prime Minister Phan Van Khai, and President Tran Duc Luong.

# A New Generation of Leadership

These three men are members of the most powerful political body in Vietnam, the fifteen-member Political Bureau (Politburo). All legislation submitted to the Vietnamese National Assembly is determined by the Politburo. In the past, the assembly simply rubber-stamped the Politburo's policies. Today, the idea of seeking consensus has been extended into the assembly, so this legislative body is slowly becoming more independent.

The assembly's more assertive role in Vietnam's politics began under Manh's leadership as chairman of the assembly during the 1950s. His skill as a consensus broker led to compromises between the assembly and the Politburo. To further boost its independence from party directives, the assembly passed a constitutional amendment under Manh's tenure giving itself the right

*Vietnam's president (left), Communist party secretary (center), and prime minister (right) meet with fellow Communist, Cuban president Fidel Castro.*

to dismiss the assembly's president and prime minister regardless of the party's wishes.

Manh's youth was an important reason for his selection as party secretary. Sixty years old when he took office, Manh was relatively young for the post. Another attractive quality Manh possesses is his minority status as a member of the Tay ethnic group. The party hopes he can help solve the many minority groups' complaints about being neglected by the government.

Above all, the party selected Manh for his impeccable reputation. The people see him as incorruptible, and the party hopes that Manh's selection will demonstrate the party's sincerity about uprooting the corruption that plagues the nation. As one Hanoi businessman puts it, "[Manh] doesn't have the army or the police in his hand. Therefore, he has to be more accountable to the people, and rely on them for support."[43]

## The Privatization of State-Owned Industry

In the past two elections to the National Assembly, the Communist Party has allowed a small number of business leaders to run. Six business leaders were elected in 2002. Bringing capitalists into the political mix demonstrates the party's realization that drastic reform toward a freer economy is needed. The party claims to have initiated a "long-term policy of developing a multi-sector market economy under State management in the direction of socialism, or in short, a socialist oriented market economy."[44] What they mean by this is that Vietnam must pass through a long period of capitalist expansion to build the economy.

The most important economic reform is privatizing industry. Until the late 1980s the government owned tens of thousands of enterprises (state-owned enterprises, or SOEs). Because most SOEs operated in the red, the government had to print money to keep them going. The resulting inflation rate peaked at 775 percent in 1986. Inflation dropped to just over 200 percent as soon as the government stopped this practice. However, more drastic measures were needed to stabilize the economy. Therefore, the government decided in the early 1990s that only state-owned enterprises that could compete successfully on the open market should continue in business.

The government could not force all SOEs to be competitive at once because most would have failed and gone out of business. Millions of people who depended on government salaries, medical coverage, and pensions would have lost their jobs. Therefore, the pace of privatizing SOEs has proceeded slowly. In the 1990s the government reduced the number of SOEs to about fifty-six hundred, and it hopes to cut this number to about two thousand by 2005.

Government officials hope to retain ownership in a core of critical industries, such as banking, power utilities, publishing, irrigation management, and air traffic control. Oil, gas, mining, railroads, and telecommunications—traditionally owned by the state—are gradually being privatized, but only after they establish themselves as profitable. The state-owned Vietnamese Posts and Telecommunications (VNPT) company, for example, operated all telephone services until 2000. Today, the Military Electronic Telecommunications Company is competing with VNPT, the first step in opening telecommunications to private firms.

## Encouraging Private Business

The party passed a law in 1990 that encouraged people to leave cooperative-run businesses and open their own private businesses. The reaction from Vietnamese entrepreneurs was dramatic: Between 1989 and 1992, the number of manufacturing cooperatives dropped from thirty-two thousand to just over thirteen thousand. They were replaced by private companies. Since then, the government has amended dozens of laws to encourage more private investment.

The CPV amended the constitution in 1992 and again in 2002 to ensure that both private and state enterprises are treated equally. A new law in 2000 removed even more obstacles to setting up businesses. Journalist Duc Hung writes that the Ministry of Trade reported that within two years "a total of 36,000 new businesses [were] set up, . . . more than the combined number of businesses registered in the previous decade."[45]

By 2002 more than a million family-owned businesses were engaged in activities such as handicrafts, trading, food processing, garment making, and transportation. Private companies generated

# Pollution

A major problem created by industrialization is environmental pollution. Industry doubled its output during the decade of the 1990s, but industrial managers have paid little attention to pollution laws, which have been on the books only since 1993. The worse offenders, according to environmental scholar David Malin Roodman in his article "Fighting Pollution in Viet Nam," are "heavy industries, such as coal mining, chemicals, and paper and pulp [that] generate half the current industrial output and probably most of the pollution." Roodman reports that a 1997 National Environment Agency survey claims that "of 9,384 major business sites nationwide, including everything from hotels to mines, half were violating the 1993 Law on Environmental Protection."

The problem in Ho Chi Minh City alone is enough to cause serious health problems for the nation. The 750 factories and enterprises and 25,000 small industries there produce 40 percent of the nation's industrial output. The pollution problem is aggravated by the 2 million motorbikes and 250,000 vehicles being run on lead-based fuel that drive the streets of Ho Chi Minh City daily. There is no quick solution to this problem except to pass environmental protection laws that allow companies to phase out inefficient production methods over decades. In 2001 the government finally began a program that would phase out the use of leaded gasoline. Vietnamese officials consider cleaning up the environment one of their top priorities as they modernize their economy.

about half of the nation's production and more than 75 percent of the nation's new jobs.

## Agricultural Reforms

Creating a vibrant business sector helps build a strong economy, but just as important to Vietnam's growth is a vigorous agricultural sector. After unification, the country's agricultural output was too low to feed even its own population. Farmers had little incentive to upgrade farming methods because they could sell surplus crops only to state-organized and regulated markets. In addition, the land belonged to the collective, an organization under party control that managed the allocation of land, the amount of crops grown, the use of equipment, the payment of government taxes, and other affairs of peasants' lives.

The real breakthrough in agriculture came during the late 1980s. Prior to that year, farmers had to till land assigned by the cooperative. However, in 1988 the government began closing agricultural cooperatives and offering farmers fifteen-year leases on the land, with the promise of renewal. Peasants could invest more time and money developing their own farms, increasing their potential production and profit. Immediately, Vietnam produced its first food surplus in decades. By the end of the twentieth century, more than 10 million households were farming their own plots and growing specialized crops for export. Vietnam became the world's second-leading exporter of rice, cashew nuts, and coffee and the leading exporter of pepper. Furthermore, food production doubled during the 1990s, helping Vietnam feed its rapidly growing population.

*A productive agricultural sector is crucial to the stability of Vietnam's economy. Here, farmers harvest rice for sale.*

# Economic Progress

The series of reforms in business and agriculture associated with *doi moi* resulted in immediate and rapid growth in the economy. By the late 1990s more than thirty thousand private enterprises competed successfully with the state-owned companies. Vietnam's economy grew at an annual rate of 7.6 percent, one of the highest in Asia. Vietnam's annual inflation rate dropped into the single digits. As the people participated more freely in Vietnam's economy, their incomes rose dramatically. During the early nineties the per capita income was approximately $220 (U.S. dollars). In 2002 this figure exceeded $400. For Ho Chi Minh City and Hanoi residents, income rose even faster, to well over $1,000 annually.

The United Nations has recognized Vietnam for its efforts to improve the living conditions of its people. In the United Nation's annual Human Poverty Index for the year 2000, Vietnam ranked forty-fifth out of ninety developing countries, compared to previous years when it ranked in the bottom third. This improvement is reflected in the huge reduction in poverty, which dropped from 50 percent in the early 1990s to around 30 percent by 2000.

# Dealing with Corruption

Vietnam's impressive accomplishments could be short-lived if officials are unable to stop the corruption that permeates all levels of government. To finalize a contract, entrepreneurs commonly pay up to 15 percent of official fees in bribes to local, provincial, and national officials. In 2002 Vietnam was considered one of the most corrupt nations in the world by Transparency International, an organization that evaluates corruption around the world.

Government officials at different levels often know ahead of time about job openings or property to be developed, and they frequently have access to files and forms that must be completed. The temptation to demand bribes for this information is often overwhelming. Historian Stanley Karnow describes how pervasive corruption has become: "Officials routinely favor wives and other relatives with contracts for supplies that, by no coincidence, are purchased by party and government bureaus. The son-in-law of one top figure, for example, has the franchise to import the computers used by the party and government." [46]

Party secretary Manh labels corruption as the major problem facing the country. A 2001 Communist Party internal investigation found that in the previous five years, sixty-nine thousand party members had been guilty of corruption. To discourage corruption, and to encourage foreign investors, Vietnam's leaders know they must establish a firm and reliable system of laws.

When *doi moi* was adopted, the government began passing laws governing foreign investment, trademarks, bankruptcy, and the environment. However, officials soon discovered that fine-tuning laws to meet the reality of life in the business world is no easy task. Many officials found ways to skirt the laws intended to eliminate corruption. As a result, the party and the National Assembly spend much of their time debating, passing, and amending laws that govern trade and commerce.

## Participating in the World Economy

Cracking down on corruption is the best way to attract foreign capital and trade. Without extensive participation by foreign companies and investors, Vietnam's economy would stagnate. Besides anticorruption laws, the government has established fifty-six industrial zones, three export processing zones, and one high-tech zone near large cities that offers foreign businesses special treatment to encourage them to move in. In addition, in 2002 Vietnam revised the Law on Foreign Investment to provide easier and quicker access to obtaining licenses, to allow companies to employ foreigners for high-level skilled jobs, and to authorize investors to deal with foreign banks.

Foreign companies are also becoming involved with Vietnam through regional and international economic organizations such as the ASEAN and ASEAN's Free Trade Area, the International Monetary Fund, the Asian Development Bank, and the World Trade Organization (WTO). These organizations facilitate trade with other nations. If Vietnam can increase its revenue from exports, the money can be used to pay off long-term loans and reinvest in

*Enlisting foreign companies like Bank of America to open offices in Vietnam has helped boost the country's economy.*

large construction projects such as updating harbors and highways. Overall, Vietnam's success in exporting products overseas has been spectacular. Between 1990 and 2001, the value of the nation's exports increased from $2.4 billion to $15.1 billion.

## Vietnamese-Russian Relations

Foreign trade in the past meant largely dealing with the Communist nations. The USSR was Vietnam's best trade partner after unification. In 1981 the two nations formed the Vietnam-Russia Oil and Gas Joint Venture (Vietsovpetro). June 1986 marked Vietsovpetro's first commercial production of oil. At the time, the company turned out approximately 95 percent of Vietnam's oil. Vietsovpetro is still Vietnam's major oil and gas company, producing about 85 percent of Vietnam's oil output in 2002.

When the Soviet Communist empire fell in the late 1980s, Russia began cutting back foreign investments. Vietnam wanted Russian oil companies to stay because oil is Vietnam's most important source of revenue (48 percent in 2002). However, a major hurdle to increasing Vietnamese-Russian trade was the large debt Vietnam owed the former USSR. In 2002 Russia agreed to restructure Vietnam's debt, reducing it by 85 percent and spreading the payments out over two decades. The Russians plan to reinvest debt payments in Vietnam and train Vietnamese specialists. In addition, Vietnam can pay off part of the debt in goods, such as rice and coffee.

## Vietnamese-Chinese Relations

Russian help is important to Vietnam's economic recovery, but even more important is trade with China. Vietnam's giant neighbor will dominate Asian trade in the future, so Vietnam needs to be on friendly terms with China. As long as the two nations were fighting each other over territory, their trade was limited. But after two decades of clashes and negotiations, they settled their long-standing border dispute in 1999. A year later they agreed to settle disputes over islands in the South China Sea and fishing rights in Bac Bo Gulf. These agreements with China have led to a rapid increase in trade, from $955 million in 1998 to more than $3 billion in 2001. China now is the second-leading importer of Vietnamese goods.

The CPV studies China's economic growth for possible ideas on how to handle Vietnam's economy. Often China's economic moves are followed soon by similar moves in Vietnam. When China entered the WTO recently, Vietnam speeded reforms to bolster its own application to join the WTO. The target date for membership is 2005.

## The U.S. Embargo

No matter how much trade Vietnam does with Russia, China, or other nations, Vietnam's long-term economic growth depends most on a healthy relationship with the United States. Creating such a relationship requires mending many past rifts. Throughout the

1980s the legacy of war undermined all attempts by either side to open talks.

The United States imposed an embargo on trade with Vietnam after that country invaded Cambodia in 1977. But the largest barrier to normal relations was the issue of the 2,238 Americans missing in action (MIA) from the war. The United States believed that Vietnamese leaders were holding back information about the MIAs. For their part, Vietnamese leaders wanted payment of the $3.25 billion in aid promised by President Nixon to get the North Vietnamese to the negotiating table during the war. Vietnam also sought compensation for the damages caused by Agent Orange, a

## The Effects of Agent Orange on Vietnam

To gain diplomatic recognition from the United States in 1995, Vietnam had to drop its demands for compensation for damages caused by Agent Orange. American forces had sprayed approximately 19 million gallons of Agent Orange on 4.5 million acres of South Vietnam's mangrove forests between 1962 and 1971 in Operation Ranch Hand in an attempt to destroy Vietcong hideouts. An estimated 14 percent of this part of coastal South Vietnam was destroyed, and scientists believe it will take at least a century to be restored.

*A Vietnamese mother holds a baby deformed by exposure to Agent Orange.*

Vietnamese officials estimate that a million people suffer from a variety of illnesses directly related to exposure to Agent Orange, which contains the highly poisonous chemical dioxin TCDD. The chemical has been linked to non-Hodgkin's lymphoma, Hodgkin's disease, and possibly to cancers of the bones and respiratory system. Some of the problems that may be linked to Agent Orange are cerebral spine defects, anencephaly, spina bifida, hydrocephaly, and learning disabilities.

chemical spray used by the United States to kill vegetation in Vietnamese forests during the war.

In 1979 Vietnam began offering some information about MIAs, so President Jimmy Carter approved Vietnam's application to the United Nations. However, during the 1980s President Ronald Reagan refused to discuss aid unless Vietnam withdrew from Cambodia and released more information about MIAs. The Vietnamese complied, and the United States began sending teams of experts to Vietnam to investigate plane crash sites.

When Vietnam withdrew from Cambodia in 1989, U.S. officials promised future trade, but this time only if Vietnam opened its economy to foreign competition and continued to cooperate on the MIA issue. Under President George H.W. Bush, the United States sold food and medicine to Vietnam, and some American businesses opened in Vietnam. Bush also promised full recognition and lifting of the trade embargo if Vietnam would begin publishing public information regarding budgets, investments, business activity, and other economic activity. All along, the United States refused to discuss the $3.25 billion and compensation for Agent Orange damage.

## Normalizing Relations with the United States

What finally persuaded the United States to drop the trade embargo was Vietnam's shift to a market-oriented economy and promises to adapt its laws to meet WTO standards. In February 1994 President Bill Clinton announced normalization of relations with Vietnam, and Congress lifted the trade embargo. Almost immediately, Pepsi and Coca-Cola were selling their products in Vietnam. Soon more than four hundred American companies, such as Mobil, Boeing, Caterpillar, and Holiday Inn, began plans to sell their products and services to Vietnam.

Further progress came in 1997, when President Clinton appointed former POW Douglas Pete Peterson as America's first ambassador to Vietnam since the war. Peterson's attitude was typical of Americans' desire to put the war behind them. He said, "I want to heal the wounds between the United States and Vietnam. It's a tragic history that we've shared as two peoples. No one can change that, but there is a great deal we can all do about the future. And that's why I'm in Vietnam."[47]

For Vietnam, the big break came in December 2001 with the Bilateral Trade Agreement (BTA). The agreement allowed for a seven-year drop in tariffs paid on imported goods by both countries. Eventually, tariffs on goods imported to the United States from Vietnam will drop from an average of 40 percent to 3 percent, enabling Vietnamese businesses to compete for the U.S. market with China and other nations.

The BTA benefited Vietnamese businesses immediately. Nguyen Huy Quang, a manager with the government-owned Garment Company Number 10, said "It was an immediate impact. The buyers saw this coming, so we had more orders immediately— much more orders. We had to open new assembly lines and expanded production by 25 percent."[48]

The new U.S. ambassador to Vietnam, Raymond F. Burghardt, described the healthy state of trade between the two nations ten months after the BTA passed: "Vietnam's exports to the United States increased by an amazing 109%—from $863 million to $1.8 billion. We fully expect that trend to continue. . . . US exports to Vietnam also increased, by 32.5%—from $366 million in the first ten months of 2001 to $485 million over the same period in 2002."[49]

## Vietnam's Future

Better educated and younger leaders changed the landscape of Vietnamese society during the 1990s. They realized their nation needed a more open, freer society to raise Vietnam out of poverty. The most obvious change has been in the economy. The vast majority of businesses are now privately owned, and their futures are determined by the free market. This new economic atmosphere has encouraged companies from the United States, Japan, China, and other nations to open branches in Vietnam. As a result of Vietnam's new market-oriented philosophy, the economy has been growing at a healthy rate.

# Vietnam in the Twenty-First Century

# 6

Vietnam in the twenty-first century is a country of the young. More than 50 million of the 80 million Vietnamese citizens are under twenty-six years old. They know nothing about the wars against France and the United States except what they studied in school. More than a third of all Vietnamese were born after *doi moi* became official policy, so their values have been formed in a society inundated with Western popular culture and values.

These young Vietnamese enter the twenty-first century facing many challenges, from inadequate education to abuses in human rights. The Communist Party leaders understand that Vietnam will gain the respect and cooperation of world nations only by making progress in these areas.

## Political Indifference

To most of the younger generation, the party has become outdated, spouting meaningless political jargon and slogans. The party's criticism that Western culture leads to the moral collapse of society was discredited after Vietnam's *doi moi* policy brought constant exposure to European and American culture. The younger generation saw how much better other people lived and blamed their nation's poverty on the Communist Party. Tuan Tran, a twenty-two-year-old Saigon motorcycle taxi driver says:

> Only after Vietnam opened up and I watched on TV and read in the magazines that I realized how rich other countries were, how amazing their movies, how beautiful their people. Then I thought of Vietnam and I felt real sad. Vietnam is a poor country compared to Thailand, Korea, and Malaysia, let alone

America. We have nothing to offer, just a nation of ignorant and malnourished people.[50]

Instead of dwelling on their nation's past, Vietnam's young people are obsessed with finding good jobs and making money. In one survey taken by the party's daily newspaper, *Nhan Dan,* young Vietnamese were asked about issues that concerned them most. The top four issues related to economics. Patriotism ranked fifth on the list. Only about 8 percent said they cared anything about politics.

One of the measures of political interest, according to the Communist Party, is membership in the Ho Chi Minh Communist Youth League. Between the late 1980s and 2000, the numbers dropped from 4.7 million to about 2.6 million. This drop reflects the common attitude that the party is irrelevant to daily life. This disregard for politics disturbs the older generation, whose members fought long, costly wars to enable their children to be free from foreign rule.

## The Influence of Popular Culture

Instead of looking to the Communist Party for inspiration, young Vietnamese are turning to popular culture from around the world for their values. They listen to popular singers from Taiwan and Hong Kong, read Japanese comics, play video games from Japan and the United States, and watch the latest American television situation comedies. Journalist William McGurn writes about a visit to Marble Mountain, a tourist spot near Da Nang. Listening in on the conversation of a dozen ten- to fifteen-year-old Vietnamese girls, he heard them "jabbering away in conversations peppered with 'okey dokey,' 'totally awesome, dude,' and 'hasta la vista, baby.'" When McGurn asked where they learned to talk this way, one of the girls confessed: "I watch too much television."[51]

Young Vietnamese have absorbed the culture of individualism from the West, which encourages people to seek self-gratification. Young couples display affections for each other openly, unconcerned about the disapproving glances from elders. The young wear Levi's jeans and Calvin Klein caps, and they carry around

*The youth of Vietnam are greatly influenced by Western culture. Here, couples display affection in public, a Western tradition new to Vietnam.*

cellular phones and pagers. To acquire these consumer items, they study for high-paying jobs in technology, computer science, and marketing. They learn English so they can land lucrative jobs with international companies. Lan To, a sales executive who earns more than seven thousand dollars a year, explains:

> Among young college students there is a saying: "First English, second informatics, and third economics. . . ." We know if there's hope for us, it's from abroad. Before the cold war ended, it's money from relatives who live in the US and Europe. Now, it's from tourism and lucrative jobs with foreign companies. Young ambitious people all want to become tour guides, sales persons, secretaries for foreign companies. [52]

The impact of Western culture extends into young people's selection of role models. In 2001 the popular magazine *Tuoi Tre (Youth)* conducted a survey of young people to discover who they admire. Of the 114 respondents, 89.5 percent listed computer mogul Bill Gates, compared to 39 percent who named Ho Chi Minh. President Bill Clinton led Premier Phan Van Khai 6.5 percent to 3.2 percent. The embarrassed government recalled the 120,000 copies and replaced the survey article. But it was too late. The survey results had already received wide circulation.

## Education

Vietnam's Communist Party realizes that to gain the respect of the young generation, it must meet their practical needs for job preparation by reforming the educational system. Students need the skills to work in high-tech industries and international business.

One of the more serious issues in education is the student dropout rate after grade five. Of the 10.3 million children (92 percent) enrolled in primary school in 2000, only about two-thirds finished grade five. Most students drop out because of the high costs for

*Improving the country's education system for students like this young girl is a high priority for Vietnam's government.*

tuition, books, and uniforms and because they need to supplement family income by working. In many cases the older child drops out when a younger brother or sister is old enough to enter first grade.

A major problem with reforming education is that 90 percent of the students attending elementary school live in rural Vietnam. Schools usually operate only part of the day, and the pressure for children to work on family farms interferes with their studies. In addition, many rural schools offer only the first two or three grades of schooling. Those who want to continue school in rural areas must travel long distances. As a result, in some parts of Vietnam—the Yen Bai and Lao Cai provinces, for example—only 10 to 15 percent of students ever go beyond grade three.

## Improving Education

One of the goals for the nation is to expand secondary education to cover more than 80 percent of eligible citizens by 2010. Predictably, the cities are more successful in meeting the nation's educational goals than rural villages. In Hanoi, for example, fewer than 2 percent of students in grades one through five drop out each year compared to 72 percent in the rural mountain province of Caobang, along the Chinese border. In Ho Chi Minh City the completion rate for grade five (primary school) is almost 96 percent. Almost all (99.7 percent) primary school graduates in Ho Chi Minh City go on to junior secondary school (grades six through nine), and their graduation rate from ninth grade is 99 percent.

Improving the attendance and graduation rate of students has led to rising educational levels for girls. Traditionally, educating girls was considered a luxury or even frivolous. Girls grew up to be wives and mothers who stayed at home serving their husbands and caring for the children. The Communists, however, have encouraged women to participate equally in society. As a result, after unification girls in urban Vietnam began to attend school in larger numbers. By the late 1980s about 82 percent of women over the age of fifteen were literate. The government renewed its campaign to reduce female illiteracy, and by the end of the twentieth century the literacy rate of women had reached about 92 percent.

## New Jobs Require Foreign Language Skills

Until the late 1980s, few jobs in Vietnam required foreign language skills. The best-paying jobs were with government-owned industries and civil service. When Vietnam began attracting foreign companies, however, new kinds of jobs opened up. These companies sought workers with fluency in English and other languages. And foreign companies paid salaries as much as 200 percent higher than those offered in government work.

Journalist Tini Tran writes that women have benefited the most from these new skill requirements. She describes one woman with an English degree, Nguyen Bich Lan, who was hired by a Hong Kong–based firm and became the human resources director within four years because of her language abilities. Lan says, "In my [university] class, there were about 25 people. Only four of them were men. Here, men are encouraged to study sciences or engineering. Foreign languages was something women chose to study more often."

As a single mother, Lan can raise her daughter comfortably on her three-hundred-dollar monthly salary. She says, "For me, knowing English made all the difference. I like the independence I have in my job and my life."

## Marriage and Family

Exposure to popular culture and modern education has not turned young Vietnamese away from their traditional ideas about family. They still express strong devotion to their parents. Scholars Russell J. Dalton and Nhu-Ngoc T. Ong report that in the World Values Survey (WVS) project, which measures social, cultural, and political attitudes around the world, 99 percent of the Vietnamese respondents said that "parents are to be respected regardless of their qualities and faults." Vietnamese also believe in the traditional role of women in the family and society: Women should be primarily mothers and housewives. According to Dalton and Ong, the WVS found that almost eight out of ten Vietnamese believe "a woman needs to have children in order to fulfill her role . . . and that being a housewife is just as fulfilling as working for pay."[53]

## Marriage and Family Reform

Not all traditional family values survived the Communist revolution, however. The custom of parents arranging marriages for their children disappeared quickly after it was outlawed in 1959. Young people were free to choose their own marriage partners. By 1962 arranged marriages were the exception.

The rights of married women received a boost in 1986 from the Marriage and Family Law, which opened the door for mixed ethnic and religious marriages and specified rights and duties within the family. Both the 1959 and 1986 laws called for equality between the sexes. However, even with their new opportunities for a better life after the late 1980s, women's progress has lagged. Advancement is obstructed by the deep-rooted values of people who judge women by how well they serve their husband and care for their children. Even today, when almost all women work outside the home to support their families, they have to do the majority of the housework when they come home. Recent figures reveal

*Traditional ideas about marriage and family remain popular in Vietnam. Here, a bride prepares for a traditional wedding ceremony.*

that women in both rural and urban Vietnam average nearly nine hours a day of outside work in addition to their five to six hours of daily housework.

## Smaller Families

The party is still trying to change the outmoded attitude toward women in society. It considers equality the morally correct position. In addition, the nation needs women to be active in the economy. But with each family averaging more than five children during the early 1980s, few women had time to work outside the home.

The government initiated a strong birth control program in the 1980s and reduced fertility rates to 3.7 children per family by 1994. The rate was still too high for steady economic growth, so the government instituted a two-child-per-family policy. In workplaces throughout the country, officials pressured women to restrict their pregnancies. However, penalties for having more than two children were hard to enforce, although among party members parents could be fined, lose their membership, and be forced to pay for health care. What has worked best is constant publicity and government pressure nationwide. By 2002 the fertility rate had been reduced to 2.3 children per family.

## Women in Politics

Changing the laws and reducing the birth rate have helped women become more active outside the home. But Vietnam's leaders are convinced that complete equality for women will only come when women's participation in the nation's politics is equal to men's.

Prior to 1975 as many as a third of the National Assembly members were women. However, the numbers declined to 18.5 percent in 1997. The party stepped in at that point and made a new commitment to bringing women back into politics. The Center for Education Promotion and Empowerment for Women, the National Committee for the Advancement of Women, and the Vietnam Women Union (VWU) have begun to train women to run in commune, district, and provincial elections. In 2002 the Asia Foundation worked closely with the VWU to offer courses that enhanced women's public speaking skills. Their efforts paid off. According to Asia Foundation, "Women's representation on People's Councils rose significantly in areas where these courses were offered—from 12 percent in 1994 to 20 percent in 1999."[54]

With the help of this training, the participation of women at all levels is rising. On People's Councils in 1999, women numbered 20.4 percent at the provincial level, 18.1 percent at the district level, and 14.4 percent at the commune (local) levels. With 27.4 percent of membership in the 2002 National Assembly, Vietnam placed ninth out of 135 nations in a world ranking of women in government. There is still a long way to go, however, before women make it to the top government positions. In 2003 women occupied only four major government positions: vice president of Vietnam, Truong My Hoa; minister of public health, Tran Thi Trung Chien; minister of labor, war invalids, and social affairs, Nguyen Thi Hang; and chairwoman-minister of the National Committee for Population, Family, and Children, Le Thi Thu.

## The Strategy for the Advancement of Women

Government efforts to improve women's status continue. In 2002 Vietnam began an extensive program called the Strategy for Advancement of Women. The plan's general objectives, to be accomplished by 2010, are "to raise the quality of women's material and spiritual life. To create all conditions for the effective exercise of women's fundamental rights as well as for the promotion of their role in all political, economic, cultural and social domains."[55]

The program details specific objectives. The first is to ensure women's equality in labor and employment. The government's goal is for half of the new jobs generated by the economy to be given to women. In addition, the government intends to expand loans to women so they can invest in businesses. Other objectives are to make sure women have equal treatment in education and to encourage a higher percentage of women to participate in higher level training and education. The government also plans to extend health care to the vast majority of women and reduce the complications occurring in pregnancies. Because of this plan and

*Vietnam's health minister Tran Thi Trung Chien is one of only four women who held a government office in 2003.*

other initiatives to promote gender equality, the United Nations has raised Vietnam's position on its Gender Development Index to eighty-ninth out of 143 nations.

## Human Rights

The Communist Party's record for promoting women's equality is commendable. However, on other human rights issues the party has a mixed record because it refuses to share political power. The party leaders maintain control by applying a simple rule to everyone: Challenging the party's authority is disloyal. The most likely people to be punished by the party are those who speak out for a multiparty political system.

International attention on human rights violations in Vietnam has reduced repression by the party in recent years. As a result, the international organization Human Rights Watch (HRW) reports that "the Vietnamese government appears keen to avoid the international . . . [disapproval] that such overt repression provokes and to prefer to use other, less obvious means to try and silence key political and religious dissidents."[56] These methods include opening mail, tapping telephone calls, and intercepting e-mail exchanges of those under suspicion. The three groups that draw the most attention are religious groups, intellectuals, and the media.

## Religious Suppression

To ensure the loyalty of religious groups, the party requires them to register with the Bureau of Religious Affairs. Six religious groups are officially recognized today: the Buddhist Church of Vietnam, with almost 7.5 million members; the Vietnamese Catholic Patriotic Association, with about 5 million; the Cao Dai Association, with nearly 5 million; the Hoa Hao Association, with about 2 million; the Protestant Christian Evangelical Church of Vietnam, with about 500,000; and the Muslim Association of Viet Nam, with about 93,000.

The government does not interfere with the religious practices of these six groups. However, several million people who worship independently in "house churches" are harassed constantly. Vietnamese law considers independent worshipers dangerous to state security.

Usually, the government persecutes the most outspoken religious leaders, such as Thadeus Nguyen Van Ly, a Catholic priest. Between 1977 and 1992 Ly served two prison terms for protesting against the government's restrictions on religions. In 2001 he was sentenced to fifteen years for arguing that the United States should ratify the Bilateral Trade Agreement only after the Vietnamese government dropped all religious restrictions. Another well-known victim of government arrest is the leader of the outlawed United Buddhist Church of Vietnam, Thich Huyen Quang. He has been under house arrest for two decades for attacking the party's policy of confiscating church land and property and for criticizing government harassment of unofficial religious groups.

## Intellectual Dissent

Throughout Vietnam's history, intellectuals have rivaled religious leaders as architects of public opinion. Therefore, intellectuals are often targeted as threats to the government. Since 1975 a long list of distinguished scientists, academics, and authors have been monitored, arrested, and imprisoned for advocating democratic reforms.

Poets and fiction writers are frequently censored. On rare occasions, the party allows a short burst of artistic freedom, but within months it slams the door shut. Historian Robert Templer explains that writers who want to follow their conscience and criticize the Socialist society usually have "to go underground or to appear in oblique metaphors that could be decoded by those in the know. By 'talking in the shadows and wind' writers could stray far beyond the boundaries." [57]

A short period of freedom flourished during the 1980s, when writers such as Duong Thu Huong, Bao Ninh, and Nguyen Huy Thiep published stories about people who were not model Socialist heroes. Both Thu Huong and Thiep served in the northern army during the 1960s and became party members. But disillusioned with the lack of freedom and economic depression after the war, they began writing about paranoid and corrupt party members and soldiers depraved by war. The government responded by restricting their travel and discouraging editors from publishing their works. Both were expelled from the party.

## Restrictions on the Media

The party monitors journalists even more closely than intellectuals. Both print and broadcast media are owned by the government and are supervised directly by the party. All journalists must register with the Ministry of Culture and Information and work for one of the ministry's licensed media organizations.

Censorship of the press has declined since the late 1980s, however. Because the nation needs foreign investments and businesses, the party allows publication of economic data. Just as important, newspapers and magazines now operate like businesses and must make a profit or fold. As a consequence, the party allows publications more latitude than ever before in story topics to attract readers. Many of Vietnam's popular newspapers, such as the *Cong An Thanh Pho Ho Chi Minh* (*Ho Chi Minh City Police Weekly*), are similar to sensational tabloids around the world, with stories about crime, entertainment, and sex.

The increased freedom of press is limited. When journalists step over the line, the party turns up the pressure on them to conform to Communist guidelines. Any call for a multiparty political system is branded as treason. In contrast, the party encourages good investigative reporting that exposes government corruption. Press exposés help party reformers catch the worst offenders and restore some public confidence in party leadership. According to deputy editor of the *Vietnam Courier* Do Le Chau:

> The change started in '84 to '85, even before renewal [*doi moi*] was officially declared. In 1985, *Tuan Tin Tic* (*Weekly News*) launched an exposé of a corruption case involving a provincial governor. At the time, we [reporters] thought the editor in chief was going to hell. Instead, the governor was stripped of his party membership, and Vietnamese journalists realized we had new power.[58]

## A Hopeful People

Even with these restraints on human rights, Vietnam has made great progress in most areas of nation building since 1990. The government has reduced poverty by 50 percent, raised literacy to almost 95 percent, and tripled per capita income. Today, most Vietnamese people appear happy with their lives. Scholars Dalton and Ong report that, according to the World Values Survey conducted by the Institute for Human Studies in Hanoi, nine out of ten Vietnamese "say they feel quite or very happy"[59] with their situation in life.

The effects of war—a polluted and scarred land, millions of broken families, and persistent poverty—are beginning to fade into the past. The people seem to approve of the direction their government is headed, according to the WVS project. Nine out of ten Vietnamese surveyed expressed confidence in their governmental institutions, although the majority hope to see their system develop more democracy.

*Life in Vietnam has improved tremendously during the past two decades, and the Vietnamese people remain hopeful about their future.*

Because the government is still not democratic, it is impossible to really know how accurately the WVS reflects the opinions of the majority. Famed novelist and dissident Duong Thu Huong, who still lives in Vietnam, distrusts studies such as the WVS. She believes that "such American study centers (that sponsored the WVS) . . . are frivolous and bureaucratic."[60] Huong says that the Hanoi government completely controls the people who are interviewed. However, the very fact that the party allows Huong to make these comments without being punished reflects a new degree of freedom in Vietnam as its leaders seek world assistance to construct a new nation out of the ruins of their twentieth-century wars.

# Notes

## Introduction: Emerging from the Shadows of War

1. Quoted in Ronald J. Cima, ed, *Vietnam: A Country Study*. Washington, DC: GPO, 1989.

2. Andrew Lam, "Clinton Will See a Vietnam That Longs for America," Pacific News Service, November 15, 2000. www.pacific news.org.

## Chapter One: Forging an Identity

3. Bernard B. Fall, *The Two Viet-Nams: A Political and Military Analysis*. 2nd rev. ed. New York: Praeger, 1968, p. 13.

4. Fall, *The Two Viet-Nams*, p. 14.

5. Quoted in *Nhan Dan*, "The Fierce Resistance of Our People: Lives of Our People Under the Nguyen," December 1, 2001. www.nhandan.org.vn.

6. Quoted in Stanley Karnow, *Vietnam: A History*. New York: Penguin, 1984, p. 107.

7. Alexander Woodside, "Vietnamese History: Confucianism, Colonialism, and the Struggle for Independence," *Vietnam: Essays on History, Culture, and Society*. Asia Society, 1985, pp. 1–20. www.askasia.org.

8. Cecil B. Currey, *Victory at Any Cost: The Genius of Viet Nam's Gen. Vo Nguyen Giap*. Dulles, VA: Brassey's, 1997, p. 20.

9. Fall, *The Two Viet-Nams*, pp. 32–33.

## Chapter Two: The Struggle for Independence

10. William J. Duiker, *Ho Chi Minh*. New York: Hyperion, 2000, p. 130.

11. Ho Chi Minh, *Ho Chi Minh Selected Writings: Part One (1920–1945)*. Hanoi: Gioi, 1994.

12. Quoted in Duiker, *Ho Chi Minh*, p. 242.

13. Quoted in Currey, *Victory at Any Cost*, p. 99.

14. Quoted in David Halberstam, *Ho*. New York: McGraw-Hill, 1987, p. 78.

15. Quoted in Ray Sarlin, "French Indochina: World War II: 1939–1945," Vietnam War Timetable, First Battalion (Mechanized), Fiftieth Infantry. www.ichiban1.org.

16. Quoted in Currey, *Victory at Any Cost*, p. 112.

17. Quoted in Duiker, *Ho Chi Minh*, p. 379.

18. Quoted in Currey, *Victory at Any Cost*, p. 135.

19. Quoted in Currey, *Victory at Any Cost*, p. 157.

20. Currey, *Victory at Any Cost*, p. 169.

21. Quoted in Currey, *Victory at Any Cost*, pp. 183–84.

**Chapter Three: The Communists Unite Vietnam**

22. Currey, *Victory at Any Cost*, p. 238.

23. Fall, *The Two Viet-Nams*, p. 250.

24. Quoted in U.S. Department of Defense, *The Pentagon Papers*. Gravel ed., vol. 1. Boston: Beacon, 1971, pp. 242–69.

25. Duiker, *Ho Chi Minh*, p. 509.

26. U.S. Department of Defense, *The Pentagon Papers*, pp. 242–69.

27. Karnow, *Vietnam*, p. 257.

28. Quoted in Fall, *The Two Viet-Nams*, p. 376.

29. Quoted in Karnow, *Vietnam*, p. 289.

30. Quoted in Karnow, *Vietnam*, p. 320.

31. Quoted in Karnow, *Vietnam*, p. 371.

32. Quoted in PBS, "Primary Sources: President Johnson and the Tonkin Gulf Incident," in "Return with Honor," *American Experience,* 1999–2000.

33. Quoted in Currey, *Victory at Any Cost,* p. 257.

34. Quoted in Stanley I. Kutler, ed., *Encyclopedia of the Vietnam War.* New York: Charles Scribner's Sons, 1996.

**Chapter Four: A Shaky Beginning**

35. Quoted in Kutler, *Encyclopedia of the Vietnam War.*

36. Quoted in Duiker, *Ho Chi Minh,* p. 478.

37. Quoted in Cima, *Vietnam.*

38. Cima, *Vietnam.*

39. Doan Van Toai and David Chanoff, "Vietnam's Opposition Today: Former Revolutionaries Turn Against the Regime," *New Republic*, April 29, 1985, p. 23.

40. Quoted in Patrick Raszelenberg, "The Khmers Rouges and the Final Solution," *History and Memory: Studies in Representation of the Past,* Fall/Winter 1999, vol. 11, issue 2, p. 62.

41. Quoted in Kutler, *Encyclopedia of the Vietnam War.*

**Chapter Five: Seeking a Place in the World**

42. David Koh, "The Politics of a Divided Party and Parkinson's State in Vietnam," *Contemporary Southeast Asia,* December 2001, vol. 23, issue 3, pp. 533–52.

43. Quoted in Margot Cohen, "Safety Valve of the People," *Far Eastern Economic Review,* April 26, 2001, n.p.

44. Communist Party of Vietnam, "Party Report Sheds More Light on Socialist Path," *Vietnam News*, February 5, 2001. www.cpv.org.vn.

45. Duc Hung, "Enterprise Law Ups and Downs," *Vietnam Investment Review,* February 18–24, 2002. www.vir.com.vn.

46. Stanley Karnow, "Vietnam Now," *Smithsonian,* January 1996, pp. 32–44.

47. Quoted in PBS, *Pete Peterson: Assignment Hanoi,* produced by Sandy Northrop, 1999. www.pbs.org.

48. Quoted in Tini Tran, "U.S.-Vietnam Trade Pact Produces Windfall in Exports for Vietnamese Business," *AP Worldstream,* December 10, 2002.

49. Raymond F. Burghardt, "Speech Presented by Raymond F. Burghardt, Ambassador, Embassy of the United States of America, Hanoi, Vietnam," Asia Society, Washington DC, chapter, International Information Programs, U.S. Department of State, January 21, 2003. http://usinfo.state.gov.

**Chapter Six: Vietnam in the Twenty-First Century**

50. Quoted in Andrew Lam, "Vietnam's Lost Generation," *San Jose Mercury News,* May 23, 1998. www.pacificnews.org.

51. William McGurn, "Good Morning, Vietnam: On the Long Road to Freedom and Prosperity, Vietnam Is Taking the First Halting Steps," *National Review,* May 15, 1995, pp. 51–56.

52. Quoted in Lam, "Vietnam's Lost Generation."

53. Russell J. Dalton and Nhu-Ngoc T. Ong, "The Vietnamese Public in Transition: The World Values Survey: Vietnam 2001," Center for the Study of Democracy, University of California, Irvine, November 9, 2001. www.democ.uci.edu.

54. Asia Foundation, "Women in Politics," 2002. www.asia foundation.org.

55. Socialist Republic of Vietnam, "Decision No 19/2002/QD-TTg of January 21, 2002, Ratifying the National Strategy for Advancement of Vietnamese Women Till 2010," *Nhan Dan,* October 16, 2002. www.nhandan.org.vn.

56. Human Rights Watch, "III. Repression of Dissident Voices," *Vietnam: The Silencing of Dissent,* May 2000, vol. 12, no. 1. www.hrw.org.

57. Robert Templer, *Shadows and Wind: A View of Modern Vietnam.* New York: Penguin, 1998, p. 181.

58. Quoted in Vikram Parekh, "Controlling Interest: Vietnam's Press Faces the Limits of Reform," Committee for the Protection of Journalists, 1996. www.cpj.org.

59. Dalton and Ong, "The Vietnamese Public in Transition."

60. Duong Thu Huong, "Interview with a Dissident," VietQuoc, December 29, 2001. www.vietquoc.com.

# For Further Reading

**Books**

Ronald J. Cima, ed., *Vietnam: A Country Study.* Washington, DC: GPO, 1989. This is the best place to start for a comprehensive review of Vietnam's history. It also includes extensive descriptions of Vietnamese society and culture, the economy, and governmental structures under the Communists.

William J. Duiker, *Ho Chi Minh.* New York: Hyperion, 2000. In this excellent biography, Duiker presents Ho Chi Minh as a charismatic leader who was willing to compromise his Communist ideology to attain support for Vietnamese independence. Duiker writes that everything about the Vietnamese revolution can be traced to Ho's activities and leadership.

Stanley Karnow, *Vietnam: A History.* New York: Penguin, 1984. Published two decades ago, Karnow's narrative is probably still the best analysis of American participation in the Vietnam War. He explains that in the Vietnamese Communists' view, their fight against the United States in South Vietnam was simply an extension of Vietnam's two-thousand-year-long struggle against foreign invaders. Karnow details what he sees as America's miscalculation of the enemy's fighting skills and determination. The book also includes a section with short biographies of more than 140 of the Vietnamese, French, and Americans mentioned in the book.

Robert Templer, *Shadows and Wind: A View of Modern Vietnam.* New York: Penguin, 1998. Templer describes Vietnamese society as desperately needing reform during the mid-1980s.

Once the government opened the nation to free enterprise, life changed dramatically. The bulk of this book details the alienation of the young, the general discontent among leading intellectuals and religious leaders, the growth of corruption throughout the country, and other problems the Communists have in controlling politics and culture.

U.S. Department of Defense, *The Pentagon Papers,* Gravel ed. Vol. 1. Boston: Beacon, 1971. Commonly known as *The Pentagon Papers,* this forty-seven volume secret Pentagon analysis of America's involvement in Vietnam after World War II was completed in 1968. The *New York Times* was able to obtain a copy of parts of the report in 1971 and began publishing excerpts with articles about the report. This is an excellent source for understanding how the U.S. government's determination to halt Communist expansion in Asia drew the United States into fighting in Vietnam.

**Websites**

*Nhan Dan*, www.nhandan.org.vn. This is the official newspaper of the Communist Party of Vietnam. It has good articles covering Vietnam's legal system, culture, history, scenery and landscapes, art, literature, folklore, food, and even a section for learning basic Vietnamese. However, the essays and photos reflect the party's desire to show only the positive side of the country to the rest of the world.

*Viet Nam News, http://*vietnamnews.vnagency.com.vn. This site covers many topics, from sports to international trade to Vietnamese economic development. It is good for general information about daily life in Vietnam, but the government does control what is published.

# Works Consulted

## Books

Cecil B. Currey, *Victory at Any Cost: The Genius of Viet Nam's Gen. Vo Nguyen Giap.* Dulles, VI: Brassey's, 1997. Currey calls General Vo Nguyen Giap one of the military geniuses in history. In this superb biography Currey describes Giap's early life and attraction to the revolution against the French being led by Ho Chi Minh. Currey explains how Giap learned the craft of warfare while fighting, not in textbooks. Giap learned from his mistakes as well. According to Currey, Giap became a logistical and strategic genius.

Bernard B. Fall, *The Two Viet-Nams: A Political and Military Analysis.* 2nd rev. ed. New York: Praeger, 1968. In great detail, Fall covers three major periods of modern Vietnam: the French colonial rule, the revolution in the north against the French, and the insurgency against the South Vietnamese government. Fall includes a detailed analysis with statistics to show what went wrong with Ngo Dinh Diem's rule, the dramatic increase of insurgency by the National Front for the Liberation of South Vietnam in the early sixties, and the steps and that drew the United States into the Vietnam War.

David Halberstam, *Ho.* New York: McGraw-Hill, 1987. This short biography is an excellent introduction to the revolutionary career of Ho, who endorsed Lenin's anticolonial version of communism. The author describes how Ho brought contesting Vietnamese Communists together to form the Indochinese Communist Party, his failed attempts to negotiate with the French after World War II, and the victory at Dien Bien Phu. The book races through the period from 1954 to Ho's death in 1969, so Ho's role in the northern policies during that period are not presented.

Stanley I. Kutler, ed., *Encyclopedia of the Vietnam War.* New York: Charles Scribner's Sons, 1996. This 750-page encyclopedia provides a comprehensive history of the Vietnam War. It includes biographies of Vietnamese, French, and American participants, descriptions of military units and campaigns, and sketches of the culture and society of Vietnam.

## Periodicals

Margot Cohen, "Safety Valve of the People," *Far Eastern Economic Review,* April 26, 2001.

Doan Van Toai and David Chanoff, "Vietnam's Opposition Today: Former Revolutionaries Turn Against the Regime," *New Republic,* April 29, 1985.

Stanley Karnow, "Vietnam Now," *Smithsonian,* January 1996.

David Koh, "The Politics of a Divided Party and Parkinson's State in Vietnam," *Contemporary Southeast Asia,* December 2001, vol. 23, issue 3.

William McGurn, "Good Morning, Vietnam: On the Long Road to Freedom and Prosperity, Vietnam Is Taking the First Halting Steps," *National Review,* May 15, 1995.

Patrick Raszelenberg, "The Khmers Rouges and the Final Solution," *History and Memory: Studies in Representation of the Past,* Fall/Winter 1999, vol. 11, issue 2.

David Malin Roodman, "Fighting Pollution in Viet Nam," *World Watch,* November 1999, vol. 12, issue 6.

Tini Tran, "English May Be Ticket to Better Job in Vietnam; Education: As the Prevailing Political Winds Turn Westward, It's the Language of Choice for Those Who Want to Move Ahead in a Career," *Los Angeles Times,* home edition, October 3, 1998.

————, "U.S.-Vietnam Trade Pact Produces Windfall in Exports for Vietnamese Business," *AP Worldstream,* December 10, 2002.

**Internet Sources**

Asia Foundation, "Women in Politics," 2002. www.asiafound ation.org.

Associated Press, "Vietnam Wrestles with Internet Growth," *USA Today,* February 3, 2003. www.usatoday.com.

Danuta Bois, "The Trung Sisters," Distinguished Women of Past and Present, 1998. www.distinguishedwomen.com.

Raymond F. Burghardt, "Speech Presented by Raymond F. Burghardt, Ambassador, Embassy of the United Statcs of America, Hanoi, Vietnam," Asia Society, Washington, DC, chapter, International Information Programs, U.S. Department of State, January 21, 2003. http://usinfo.state.gov.

Anita M. Busch, "'Traitor' Leaves Vietnam for U.S.," *Los Angeles Times,* April 8, 2003. http://perso.wanadoo.fr.

Communist Party of Vietnam, "Party Report Sheds More Light on Socialist Path," *Vietnam News,* February 5, 2001. www.cpv. org.vn.

Russell J. Dalton and Nhu-Ngoc T. Ong, "The Vietnamese Public in Transition: The World Values Survey: Vietnam 2001," Center for the Study of Democracy, University of California, Irvine, November 9, 2001. www.democ.uci.edu.

Duc Hung, "Enterprise Law Ups and Downs," *Vietnam Investment Review,* February 18–24, 2002. www.vir.com.vn.

Human Rights Watch, "III. Repression of Dissident Voices," *Vietnam: The Silencing of Dissent,* May 2000, vol. 12, no. 1. www.hrw.org.

Duong Thu Huong, "Interview with a Dissident," VietQuoc, December 29, 2001. www.vietquoc.com.

Andrew Lam, "Clinton Will See a Vietnam That Longs for America," Pacific News Service, November 15, 2000. www.pacific news.org.

———, "Vietnam's Lost Generation," *San Jose Mercury News,* May 23, 1998. www.pacificnews.org.

Lam Le Trinh, "The Youth of Vietnam Holds the Key to the Rebirth of the Nation," *VietForum.* http://vietforum.org.

*Nhan Dan,* "The Fierce Resistance of Our People: Lives of Our People Under the Nguyen," December 1, 2001. www.nhandan. org.vn.

Vikram Parekh, "Controlling Interest: Vietnam's Press Faces the Limits of Reform," Committee for the Protection of Journalists, 1996. www.cpj.org.

PBS, *Pete Peterson: Assignment Hanoi.* Produced by Sandy Northrop, 1999. www.pbs.org.

———, "Primary Sources: President Johnson and the Tonkin Gulf Incident," in "Return with Honor," *American Experience,* 1999. www.pbs.org.

———, *Vietnam Passage: Journeys from War to Peace.* Produced by Sandy Northrop, 2002. www.pbs.org.

Ray Sarlin, "French Indochina: World War II: 1939–1945," Vietnam War Timetable, First Battalion (Mechanized), Fiftieth Infantry. www.ichiban1.org.

Socialist Republic of Vietnam, "Decision No 19/2002/QD-TTg of January 21, 2002, Ratifying the National Strategy for Advancement of Vietnamese Women Till 2010," *Nhan Dan,* October 16, 2002. www.nhandan.org.vn.

Alexander Woodside, "Vietnamese History: Confucianism, Colonialism, and the Struggle for Independence," *Vietnam: Essays on History, Culture, and Society.* Asia Society, 1985. www.askasia.org.

# Index

# Picture Credits

# About the Author

Tony Zurlo has taught in Nigeria with the Peace Corps and at a teacher's university in China. He lives in Arlington, Texas, with his wife, an artist and educator from China. His publications include the nonfiction books *Immigrants in America: Japanese Americans; Japan: Superpower of the Pacific; China: The Dragon Awakes; Indigenous People of Africa: West Africa; Daily Life in Hong Kong;* and *Nations in Transition: China.* Zurlo's poetry, fiction, reviews, and essays have appeared in over sixty literary magazines, newspapers, and anthologies.